ERDDIG

Wrexham

THE NATIONAL TRUST

Acknowledgements

Merlin Waterson's *The Servants' Hall* (1980) has justly become
a modern classic among country house books, exploring the
complex lives of the Erddig servants over three centuries in
unsentimental detail. That book could hardly be bettered, but
the Erddig archives are so rich that they can tell many stories.
This new guide therefore has a more conventional focus – on
the owners of Erddig and the house they built, furnished,
decorated and then hung on to against the odds. It is also
deeply indebted to the research notes, writings and advice of
Gervase Jackson-Stops. The picture entries were compiled
from Alastair Laing's detailed notes, and the ceramics entries
by Anthony du Boulay; the rest of Chapter Six and the whole
of Chapter Eight were written by Jane Gallagher; the history
of the park and garden in Chapter 7 was written by
Christopher Gallagher; the tour section is based on a guide
written by Jonathan Marsden. I am grateful to A. Geoffrey
Veysey and his colleagues at the Clwyd Record Office for
their help, and would also like to thank Robert Dillon, the
former Property Manager at Erddig, and Jeremy Cragg, the
House Manager, for their patient responses to numerous
inquiries.

OLIVER GARNETT

Photographs: Clwyd Record Office p. 6; Country Life Picture Library
p. 29; National Trust pp. 7, 23, 26, 27, 60, 78, 80, 86, 87, 89, 90, 91, 92;
NT/Christopher Gallagher p. 85; National Trust Photographic
Library pp. 15 (above right), 25, 33, 43, 79; NTPL/John Bethell pp. 32,
35, 46; NTPL/Andreas von Einsiedel pp. 10, 15 (below left), 36, 37, 38,
39, 40, 41, 44, 45, 47, 48, 50, 51, 52, 53, 55, 57, 62, 66, 69, 70, 72, 75, 76,
back cover; NTPL/Barry Hamilton p. 94; NTPL/John Hammond
front cover, pp. 1, 9, 13, 14, 17, 19, 20, 21, 22, 42, 49, 56, 59, 63, 68, 73, 83;
NTPL/Rupert Truman pp. 4, 16, 77, 84; John Sergeant/Foundation
for Art, NTPL/John Hammond p. 64.

First published in Great Britain in 1995 by the National Trust
© 1995 The National Trust
Registered charity no. 205846

ISBN 0 7078 0197 4

Reprinted with corrections 1999, 2001; revised 2002

Designed by James Shurmer

Phototypeset in Monotype Bembo Series 270
by SPAN Graphics Ltd, Crawley, West Sussex (SG1643)

Print managed by Centurion Press Ltd (BAS)
for the National Trust (Enterprises) Ltd,
36 Queen Anne's Gate, London SW1H 9AS

CONTENTS

The central nine bays of the garden front formed Joshua Edisbury's original house, built by Thomas Webb in 1684

CHAPTER ONE

JOSHUA EDISBURY

In 1682 Joshua Edisbury was appointed High Sheriff of Denbighshire; it was to be the making of Erddig, and the unmaking of Edisbury.

The Edisbury family had been minor gentry in the county since at least the mid-sixteenth century. Joshua's father, John, was a local barrister and steward to Sir Thomas Myddelton at nearby Chirk Castle. Joshua himself was a generous, easy-going man, fond of gambling on cock-fights and always ready to bail out family and friends when they were short of money, which was often. Not surprisingly, his appointment as High Sheriff was popular in the county. The family home at Pentre Clawdd, solid and sensible though it was, must have seemed too humble for his new status, as the following year he decided to build a new house.

Edisbury chose a dramatic site on an escarpment above the winding River Clywedog a mile south of Wrexham. There seems to have already been a house here, but all trace of it was swept away by the new building. On 1 November 1683 Thomas Webb, freemason of Middlewich in Cheshire, 'covenanted and agreed to undertake and perform the care and oversight of the contriving, building and finishing of a case or body of a new house'. The bricks were laid by William Carter of Chester; the stone was supplied by Edward Price. Work began in 1684. Webb estimated for 'a house 85 foot long and 50 foot deepe' to a design that had been pioneered by Sir Roger Pratt in the 1660s and had since become widely popular for British country houses: two storeys and a basement beneath a single, hipped roof and topped by a central cupola and four tall chimneystacks. The unornamented windows originally had timber casement frames, the mullions of which still survive in the basement storey. The outward appearance of Webb's house is best seen today in the central nine bays of the east, garden front, where Price's pedimented central doorcase

provides the only embellishment. The plan followed the 'double-pile' form recommended by Pratt – two sets of rooms set back-to-back and divided by symmetrically arranged main and back stairs. Although some of the internal partitions were tinkered with by Edisbury's successors, his original conception has survived remarkably little altered.

In his estimate, Webb noted: 'The plastering I have here omitted because some of ye Rooms may be wainscotted and other inferior Rooms not plastered at all.' The deeply moulded panelling which is still such a feature of Erddig was left to Philip Rogers, a carpenter from Eyton, but he was late with the work, and in September 1686 was obliged to 'promise [that the staircase] shall be completed & finished by ye 15th April next ensuing. The hall to be layd (out of hand) with deal, and after to be layed wth oak; ... ye great parlour to be lay'd wth oak.' After the woodwork was finally completed, much of it was painted or grained in a variety of colours by the exotically named White Crisp Burtch of Nantwich, as Edisbury's agent reported in July 1692:

Concerning the rooms, the drabe roome I think is painted very well the pannells are resembling Yew, the stiles to prince wood [a dark-coloured, light-veined West Indian wood], and the moulding a light color. The Doctor's Chamber [used by Joshua's brother, John] is pretty well don sumewhat like Ash, I think; and vained much like the Hall. The other roome is but ordinary, I think, and plane, ether a dark browne or sumewhat like sinnimone culor.

According to John Prince, a witness at Edisbury's trial in 1715, 'All the harthes and chimneys are curiously fitted some with Marble and others with freestone.' These may have been the chimneypieces put up by Edward Price, but in January 1693 William Leeke of Apley Castle offered Edisbury new chimneypieces made from 'a pretty sort of

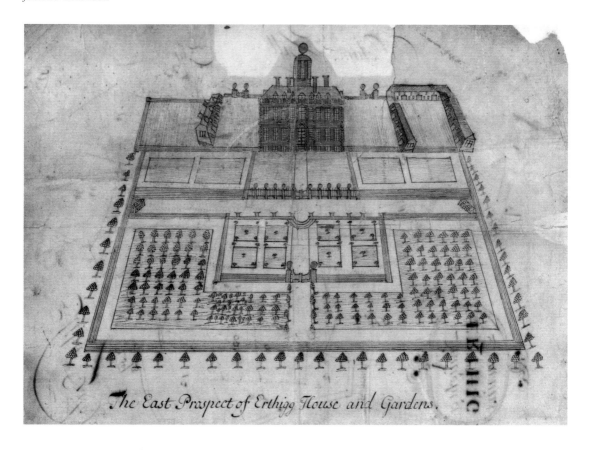

The Erddig survey of c.1713 shows the east front and formal garden of Edisbury's house

marble' he had discovered near Doddington Hall, the Cheshire home of Edisbury's wife, Grace Delves.

We know almost nothing about how Edisbury furnished his new house: the 'full inventory' made around 1709 has, alas, disappeared. In 1694 he bought a pair of silver-mounted tables and 'a large flagon' from the London goldsmith Alexander Pulford, but after Edisbury's fall these and the rest of the contents were all sold, bar a few things put aside in 'the Blue Closet'. According to family tradition, they included the remarkable six-panel screen of incised lacquer (now in the State Bedroom), which was said to have been given him by Elihu Yale. Today Yale is famous as the benefactor of the American university that bears his name, but in the 1680s he was governing Fort St George at

Madras for the East India Company. Edisbury was eager to curry favour with such a rising man, who had been brought up on the neighbouring estate at Plas Grono. So he decided to present him with 'four Rundletts [casks] of Sandpatch Ale' – 74 gallons in all. On 20 April 1682 Yale wrote back a letter of effusive and rather stilted thanks, sending to Edisbury in return a cask of 'our best mango Atchar [chutney]' and to his wife 'A Japan Skreen'.

In 1684 Webb had estimated that Edisbury's new house would cost £677 10s 9d to build. This was hardly a vast sum, when one considers that the mason-contractor William Stanton was paid around £5,000 between 1685 and 1688 to erect Belton House in Lincolnshire. But fitting up and furnishing the building, and laying out the elaborate formal garden (see Chapter Seven) must have cost a great deal more, if John Prince was right when he testified in 1715 that the total bill was over £8,000.

It was certainly more than Edisbury could afford. His relations continued to pester him for money, his investments in the lead mines at Gop and Trelogan in Flintshire began to turn sour, and he had to borrow more simply to pay off the interest on old debts. By the late 1690s he was in dire financial straits and turned to Elihu Yale for help. Their former friendship evaporated when Yale, who had been forced to leave Fort St George after accusations of extortion and murder, demanded £4,000 in payment for a loan of half that. Edisbury's servants at Erddig remained remarkably loyal, but the miners at Trelogan became understandably restive when their wages went unpaid, despite repeated pleas to Edisbury from the mine agent. Finally, George Williams wrote in despair in October 1696:

I declare I never knew soe small a Concern as yrs. at Trelogan is in soe great a Confusion, for ye workmen have almost all run away and those few wch are left will not touch the sough [mine drain] upon ye former terms.

Joshua's brother, Dr John Edisbury, a successful lawyer, MP for Oxford University and, from 1684, a Master in Chancery, came to his aid, but only succeeded in being ruined with him. John was found to have stolen Chancery fees in a vain attempt to stave off his brother's creditors, and was brought to trial. In May 1712 he signed a petition to the Lord Chancellor which spelt out the brothers' plight very clearly:

[he] doth with the Utmost Shame & Sorrow acknowledge his Crimes and abhor himselfe for his breach of Trust in missaplying the money by the Orders of this Court comitted to his Charge, so that he is at present unable to pay ye same.

But forasmuch as your Pet[itione]^r was Seduced into that Guilt by affection to his Brother whose Estate yor Pet^r *then verily believed* to be more than sufficient to reimburse the money lent, and all other Incumbrances whatsoever . . .

Dr Edisbury died in disgrace the following year; Joshua, who had been declared bankrupt in 1709, left Erddig for ever and seems to have spent the rest of his life in London. He is last heard of in 1716, when he was living 'at the Blew Spires in the Old Bayley'. After that, silence.

In Edisbury's absence, the house was let out to a Mr Alport. The principal mortgage on the estate was held by Dr Edisbury's Chancery superior, the Master of the Rolls Sir John Trevor, who was also a member of one of the oldest families in Denbighshire. Trevor's reputation for political duplicity was not helped by a ferocious squint. He certainly did not endear himself to John Williams, the Erddig steward, who reported to Edisbury the gradual dissolution of all that he had created with a mixture of sadness and loyal efficiency. Like the housekeeper Elizabeth Lea and the rest of the staff, Williams did his best to adjust to the new regime, but was peremptorily rebuffed when he tried to show Trevor round in September 1709:

I ask'd his honour if he would be pleased to see the other Gardens (no) and when he came in I asked if he pleased to see the house (no) I also ask'd him if he would be pleased to drink anything that I had which he pleased viz. wine or Clarett (no).

John Williams left the Edisburys' employ that month; it is typical of the man that he should have written to Mrs Edisbury apologising for the distress his departure had caused her.

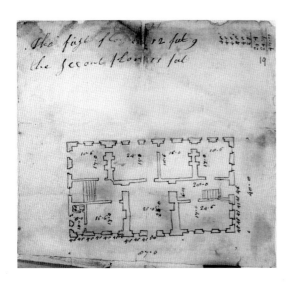

An undated plan of the main floor of Edisbury's house

CHAPTER TWO
JOHN MELLER

On 28 January 1714 John Meller became the 'best purchaser' of Erddig, having offered £17,000 for the estate. However, it was not until August 1716 that he finally succeeded in buying out Sir John Trevor. Meller came from a Derbyshire family and had grown rich as a barrister in the Middle Temple; indeed he succeeded John Edisbury as Master in Chancery after his disgrace. However, in almost every other respect, Meller was a different character from the Edisburys. He was plain-spoken and 'not apt to flatter his Freinds', as one of his pupils put it. Meticulous in accounting for every penny he spent, he coolly rebuffed the claims of needy relatives. His sister Aliza thought him 'hard-laced'. When his brother-in-law Simon Yorke's wholesale grocery business got into difficulties, he wrote:

You must have known long since what way is the custom of the Queens Bench, and therefore if there was a necessity for the Money you should have applyed to your own relations and provided in time for it. For my part I find Money scarce enough with all my outgoings.

Simon ended up in debtors' prison, and his spend-thrift son John Yorke was obliged to seek his fortune abroad, having apologised that 'the chiefest of my Extravagancy has been in Books'.

When Meller finally acquired the estate, he was already 51, but still a bachelor, and therefore a promising catch. Joshua Edisbury's sister Martha Lloyd sought to rescue the family's position in the county by marrying him off to her daughter Patty. Nothing came of the match, and Meller remained single, with a sister acting as housekeeper at Erddig in the early days. In 1732 the antiquary John Love-day remarked that Meller was 'not very agreeable to ye Countrey'. His part in the downfall of a popular local figure must still have rankled. As a fierce anti-Jacobite, he was also politically out of sympathy with many of the Denbighshire gentry; indeed in

1731 the beleaguered Prime Minister Robert Walpole was keen to offer him any help he could against the local Tory magnates.

John Meller may have been an unlovable man, but he was neither a miser nor a philistine. He owned a large London house in the fashionable quarter of Bloomsbury Square, for which Sir James Thornhill designed a *trompe-l'oeil* portico. When he bought Erddig, he found the house almost bare, but at once set about furnishing it 'in yᵉ grandest manner, & after yᵉ newest fashion', according to Loveday. Thanks to Meller's meticulous accounting and an inventory of 1726, we are able to envisage his interiors and document in unusual detail his superb furniture, much of which still survives at Erddig. Loveday was suitably impressed after his visit in 1732:

Above Stairs a Gallery hung wᵗʰ yᵉ Sibylls, all lengths [twelve in all]. The Stair-case & Rooms are wains-cotted wᵗʰ Oak, & have yᵉ convenience of Dressing Rooms, & Rooms for Servants. They are furnish'd wᵗʰ Mohair, Coffoy [caffoy – a cut-wool velvet], Damasks, &c. The grand Apartments are below Stairs [ie on the ground floor].

Loveday's tour of the 'grand Apartments' would have begun with the Entrance Hall in the centre of the west front. Here and in most of the principal rooms there were new marble chimneypieces and window seats commissioned from the sculptor Robert Wynne of Ruthin, who was also working in the 1720s for the Myddeltons at Chirk. A gilded leather screen helped to keep out the draughts, which have always been a problem in this room. As a room of passage, there was little need for other furniture: in 1726 there were ten leather black hall-chairs pushed back against the walls, two marble-topped pier-tables and a large Dutch table. The Entrance Hall also seems to have been used as a games room, with a pair of backgammon tables and

nobis hæc otia fecit.

John Meller of Erthig Esq
one of the Masters of the High Court
of Chancery ob. 1733 ætat 68

John Meller (1665–1733), who bought Erddig in 1716 and filled it with superb furniture; possibly by Charles Jervas,
c.1715 (Dining Room). Gainsborough reworked the picture in 1780

a three-cornered table at which to play ombre, a three-handed card game popular in the early eighteenth century.

The Hall was flanked, on the right, by the Eating Parlour (now the Drawing Room), which had crimson silk curtains and a tea-table, together with all the implements needed for making and serving tea. This room catches the afternoon sun. (There was a separate room for breakfast upstairs.) To the left was the Little Parlour (now the Library), which had tasselled green curtains, a square Dutch table and one of the few pictures in the house. Loveday mentions 'an excellent picture of ye Virgin & Babe' and 'a good Picture of a jocose Frier'.

Having left his hat on the brass stand in the passage by the back stairs, Loveday would have crossed the Hall and passed through a central door (now gone) into the Saloon – the typical late seventeenth-century arrangement. One should imagine Meller's Saloon two-thirds its present size and dominated by a set of eight walnut side-chairs and settee. With their exceedingly rare dark crimson and yellow caffoy loose covers, they were designed to match the crimson and yellow curtains that once hung here. This was only the first example of carefully co-ordinated colour schemes of increasing sumptuousness and complexity.

Loveday remarked on the 'very fine Glasses' at Erddig. Meller certainly seems to have been fond of his own reflection. For throughout the principal rooms there is mirror glass everywhere, in frames by the finest London makers of the day. The smaller pair of sconces still in the Saloon, with their gilt gesso frames and glass candle branches, was supplied for this room in 1720 by John Pardoe, whose workshop near Temple Bar in the Strand made and sold 'all sorts of Looking Glasses, Couch Glasses, Cabinet Work & Chairs, Beds & Bedding wth all other sorts of Goods in the Cabinet & Upholstere^{rs} way'. In 1726 these mirrors probably hung above '2 Marble Tables with Walnutree Fraims' (now gone).

(Right) The silver pier-glass was made for Meller by John Belchier in 1723 to hang with the silvered furniture in the Withdrawing Room. It is now in the Tapestry Room above a pier-table supplied in 1726

Following Baroque convention, the principal apartment was entered from the Saloon and occupied the south-east corner of the ground floor. The first in this suite of increasingly private and lavish rooms was the Withdrawing Room, which today is part of the Saloon. Silver and crimson set the note for the furnishings. The set of eight side-chairs and settee, 'ye frames of wch are plated with Silver', was upholstered in flowered crimson Spitalfields velvet, to match the crimson velvet curtains and window cushions. A silvered table, topped with mirror glass and with 'Mr Millar's Arms work'd in y^e middle',

came in 1726 from the workshop of John Belchier in St Paul's Cathedral churchyard. (At this time Belchier was also making new glass for the cathedral.) To hang on the pier above, he supplied a 'Large Sconch with a Silver Frame & 2 pairs of Glass Arms'. Both table and sconce are now in the Tapestry Room. Another silver-framed mirror (now gone) hung over the chimneypiece.

Beyond was the climax of the suite, the Best Bedchamber (now part of the Dining Room). Here the main colours were green, white and gold, the mood exotic. Dominating the room was the State Bed, superbly fitted out with white Chinese embroidered silk hangings by a 'Mr Hurt'. This was probably John Hutt, who had workshops near Belchier in St Paul's churchyard. Belchier himself seems to have been responsible for the fabulous carved and gilded hawks' heads on the bed-head. Between November 1722 and January 1726 Meller spent no less than £262 16s on furniture from Belchier. Again, there were matching curtains and window cushions in embroidered white silk. The foreign flavour of the bed was taken up in the three Soho tapestries that hung round the room (those now in the Tapestry Room), which featured oriental scenes. The antiquarian Loveday was particularly taken with 'Hen. 8th's Dressing Table . . . of Tortoise-Shell thick-inlaid with fine Brass' (now in the Saloon). This ambitious provenance is typical of Erddig: the table is actually late seventeenth-century and French – one of the earliest documented examples of Louis XIV Boullework in Britain. Above was another of Belchier's gilt pier-glasses, surmounted by grotesque gilt masks and curling foliage (also now in the Saloon). In it would have been reflected the glowing colours of '6 gold stuff chairs with green japan frames' and '2 gold stuff stools and green japan frames' (now in the State Bedroom).

There was plenty more furniture lacquered in red, green and black in the rest of the house. The most spectacular surviving piece is the gilt and scarlet japanned bureau-cabinet, probably made by Belchier (now also in the State Bedroom). If the outside was as vibrant a scarlet as the inside is today, then it must have made a truly dazzling impact among the largely blue furnishings of the 'Blew Mohair Room'. The upstairs furnishings were in general plainer, walnut pieces with less spectacular textiles than those in the rooms below. The main room on the first floor was the panelled gallery. Although the paintings of Sibyls noted by Loveday have gone, it has otherwise changed little, still running across the centre of the house from east to west. Similar axial galleries were once to be found in the slightly earlier Kingston Lacy in Dorset and Wimpole Hall in Cambridgeshire.

In 1732 Loveday ended his tour of the house with the words: 'The Chappel is not quite finish'd, yᵉ pews &c. Oak.' This is perhaps explained by the fact that the Chapel occupies one of the wings that Meller added between 1721 and 1724 to link Edisbury's house and outlying pavilions. Meller, who may have been his own architect, added two-storey wings of two bays to north and south, with oval 'bull's-eye' windows and open arcades on the west front. He left the exterior of the central block as Webb had built it, apart from inserting more fashionable sash-windows on the first and second floors and putting up new front steps. Badeslade's bird's-eye view (illustrated on p.80) shows the result. Apart from the Chapel, the new wings also allowed more space for proper dressing-rooms and closets off the main bedchambers – an improvement that met with Loveday's approval. Most of the new work seems to have been completed by 1724, when Meller's steward, Richard Jones, wrote to him: 'Since your Honour lef Erthig there has been 4 Coaches full of Gentry to see the Hall . . . they all admired the Hall and furniture Mitily.'

Meller did not have much longer to enjoy his newly furnished house. In 1726 he was already complaining of his 'indifferent state of health which makes business troublesome', and by the early 1730s his eyesight was failing. His sister Anne recommended the herb Eyebright as a remedy: 'I had the distilled water of it and thought it no way unpleasant being sweetened with sugar you may also make a tea of it or have it dried powdered to take in any manner you please.' It can have brought only temporary relief, as on 23 November 1733 he died. His memorial by Peter Scheemakers in Marchwiel church bears a simple Latin inscription, which ends with a plea for resurrection: '*Resurgam*'.

CHAPTER THREE

SIMON I AND PHILIP I YORKE

Who would inherit Erddig? Meller had no children and no very high opinion of his relatives – apart from his sister Anne, who came to live at Bloomsbury Square after the death of her husband in 1723. Meller looked to her younger son Simon in London to supervise the prompt completion and delivery of his valuable new furnishings for Erddig. Simon Yorke signed himself 'your most Dutiful Nephew', and so he proved, writing to his uncle in December 1720: 'The Tapestry Weaver called here, to acquaint me that ye other piece of Tapestry was finish'd. . . . I shall not now send it into ye Country without order because I believe that ye Roads being full of water the Tapestry may possibly receive damage.' The Soho tapestries arrived safely; indeed Meller was so pleased with his nephew's efficiency that he bequeathed Erddig to him.

The epitaph on Simon Yorke's monument in Marchwiel church calls him 'a pious temperate country Gentleman, of a very mild, just and benevolent character, as the concern for his death did best testify; An Advantage which Amiable Men have over great Ones.' He was certainly not to be numbered among the 'great Ones' like his cousin, Philip Yorke, 1st Earl of Hardwicke, who was Lord Chancellor from 1737 to 1756. He was content to enjoy his good fortune, developing the garden at Erddig (see Chapter Seven), but doing little to the house. It was only after a certain amount of good-humoured chivvying from his lawyer friends that in 1739, at the age of 43, he decided to marry the nineteen-year-old Dorothy Hutton, heiress to her brother James's Hertfordshire estate of Newnham. An engraved glass beaker in the Saloon celebrates their marriage.

In May 1740 Simon brought his new wife back to Wales; a neighbour observed the scene: 'Everybody's eyes was fixed and all their attention upon his young Bride, who acquited herself soe well at that time [in her] then publick station that she gained the Applause of everybody.' She could relax with a game of billiards at the table which was installed in 1742 in what is now the Tribes Room. 'I hope', one of Simon Yorke's friends wrote, 'that Mrs Yorke is become proficient in the skill of pocketing.' However, she seems to have found running Erddig a struggle. Disagreements about the servants' wages caused her sleepless nights, 'but whilst I keep house I shall never pinch my Servants. A large house in Wales is the worst thing in the world to manage.' She longed for a smaller, more convenient home in London, but her mother-in-law continued to occupy the Bloomsbury Square house until her death in 1748, and the Yorkes seem to have visited the capital only rarely after their marriage. Instead they rented a house in Chester during the winter, when Erddig was closed up.

On 29 July 1743 their only son was born. It is perhaps to Philip Yorke more than anyone that Erddig owes its special character. Although he was the first owner to have been born on the estate, he spent much of his early life away from Denbighshire, at schools in Wanstead in Essex and then in Hackney. Phil, as his mother called him, was a cheerful, precocious child. An avid reader from an early age, he was fond of the theatre and of dressing up; at five he was already asking his mother to send his favourite silver waistcoat, and at the same age he decided to become a vegetarian. A sister, Anne Jemima, did not arrive until he was eleven. She was delicate, musical and doted on by her mother, who splashed out on a Jacob Kirkman harpsichord for her in 1769. After a year at Eton, Philip went up to Cambridge in 1762, where he was an industrious student and, like most students, critical of his teachers, whose lectures he thought 'neither extraordinary clever or Entertaining'. He found the 'concise and laconick Stile' of Tacitus 'peculiarly obscure, at least to my Faculty of resolving', but was keen to take on a private tutor to improve matters. He was soon writing long letters to his father discoursing learnedly on Locke's *Essay concerning Human Understanding*. 'Your father is tired', his mother reported anxiously, and in 1767 Simon Yorke died, when Philip was 23. He seems to have left his mother to look after Erddig, while he remained in London at Lincoln's Inn, where he had just been called to the Bar.

Philip's closest friend at Cambridge had been Brownlow Cust, the son of Sir John Cust of Belton in Lincolnshire, the Speaker of the House of Commons. Around 1767 he fell in love with Brownlow's sister, Elizabeth. There was, however, one major obstacle to the match – Philip's uncle, James Hutton. Philip and the whole of his family were acutely aware that his future prospects, and even perhaps the future of Erddig, depended on securing Hutton's inheritance, and that depended on getting his approval for the marriage. The first

Simon Yorke I (1696–1767), painted around the time he inherited Erddig, in 1733; attributed to Edward Wright (Dining Room)

signs were not encouraging, and as a result Sir John Cust started to get cold feet. Brownlow Cust revealed his father's anxieties to Philip in September 1767:

And when I hinted to him Mr H's disapprobation of your marrying, it struck him very much. He has been taught from his infancy so much to dread divisions in a family, that he wou'd fear very much for his daughter marrying into one that was divided. And as to fortune he apprehends there wou'd scarcely be a sufficiency between you.

On Sir John's approval rested Elizabeth's dowry of £10,000. In January the following year Philip steeled himself to visit his uncle at Newnham. After an agonising wait, finally, at 10 o'clock on the last evening, Hutton revealed his intentions. He said that his only objection had ever been his nephew's lack of fortune. (Philip restrained himself from pointing out that it was in his uncle's power to remove that objection at a stroke.) Hutton confirmed, 'My Fortune I have made to descend to. you,' although at the same time 'he muttered – that I treated the Expectancy from him more familiarly than it might deserve.' Their conversation went on till one in the morning, but at last Philip was able to report to his prospective father-in-law: 'I am now totally delivered from all apprehensions of my Uncle's displeasure.' Nevertheless, the next two years were a period of intense anxiety for Philip. Could his uncle be relied on not to revoke the will? As Dorothy Yorke is said to have remarked at the time, 'My poor brother is dying slowly of drunkenness and debauchery, and when I remonstrate with him he damns my eyes.' Hutton had a mistress living in his London house in Park Lane, and a sinister character named Chilton hovered in the background, who might persuade him in a moment of weakness to change his mind.

In the end Philip and Elizabeth decided to get married anyway, on 2 July 1770. The final months of their engagement were darkened by the deaths of Elizabeth's father and then, at only sixteen, of Anne Jemima. For the Yorke and Cust families it was to be a year of two weddings and three funerals – perhaps the most important year in Philip Yorke's life. They need not have worried: when Hutton died shortly after the wedding, his will was found to

Philip Yorke I (1743–1804); painted by Thomas Gainsborough, probably in the late 1770s (Dining Room)

be unaltered. Philip inherited not only the Newn-ham estate but also a fine collection of pictures and china, including the famous late seventeenth-century Delft orange-tree pot now in the Tapestry Room. Most of these remained in the Park Lane house, where Dorothy spent the rest of her long widowhood, until her death in 1787. She had got her wish for comfortable London lodgings, which she shared with her maid, Betty Ratcliffe. Betty created a series of astonishingly intricate models from mica, mother-of-pearl and glass, which were cherished by successive generations of Yorkes and now stand in the Gallery (see p.68).

With the Hutton inheritance and Elizabeth's dowry, the Yorkes were able to start doing up

Elizabeth Cust (1750–79), who married Philip Yorke I in 1770; by Francis Cotes (Dining Room)

Erddig, which was now almost 100 years old. Even before they were married, Elizabeth had begun to order new furnishings. In March 1770 she wrote to her fiancé:

I am peculiar in one thing, I hate to be disappointed ... I have (perhaps not done wisely) not cut my Coat according to my Cloth, but my Cloth to my room; I have got quantity of *charming* Chintz, you must not be angry, you cannot with me.

And the following day:

Tradespeople of every sort are most tiresome to deal with – I sent several messages after my Chair since I wrote, but not receiving satisfaction, I went myself yesterday, ... all I could get for my trouble was to hear it was impossible to be done. ... One must have some-body to scold (as it is a very constitutional exercise) and a Cabinet maker as well as any. Whilst I am in this humour (ie out of humour) don't expect to escape tho' so distant; I did expect the account how much paper would be wanted for the *new* dressing Room.

(Left) The Chinese Pagoda, made by Betty Ratcliffe in 1767 (Gallery)

The west front, which was refaced in stone in 1772

In 1771 more major alterations began. Philip Yorke was not a man to make changes merely for the sake of fashion. He left the garden front as he found it, but the brickwork of the west front, exposed to the prevailing winds, seems to have needed attention, so he decided to recase the whole front in stone. The first block was laid in April 1772 by the mason William Worrall. However, there is some uncertainty about who was responsible for the design. A local Shropshire architect, William Turner of Whitchurch, was paid for replacing the arcades and 'bull's-eye' windows in Meller's wings with new sash-windows, and Turner's cousin Joseph and a Mr Franks were also consulted. But among the Erddig papers are a payment dated January 1774 to James Wyatt, an undated memorandum headed 'Subjects to take Mr Wyatt's opinion upon', and an elevation drawing

for the west front, which seems to be in Wyatt's hand. Wyatt was still in his twenties, but had already made a national reputation. He was also both busy and dilatory, and it seems unlikely that he was closely involved. The changes he proposed were very similar to those he was to make in 1776 at Belton – another house of the 1680s – for Elizabeth's brother. Some were accepted: a three-bay pediment was put up, and the cupola removed. But Philip baulked at reducing the wings to single-storey arcades lined with Doric columns and flanked by pedimented pavilions. The result, it has to be admitted, is rather unsatisfactory. The stone chosen was dour and the lack of any window ornament gives the façade a distinctly barracks-like quality. For this we may perhaps blame Joseph Turner, who later built gaols at Ruthin and Flint.

Wyatt also advised on the new stableyard, spacious kitchen and other domestic offices that were laid out to the south of the house and completed in

1774, as the date-stone over the entrance arch proclaims. But, again, the work seems to have been put in local hands; he can hardly have been responsible for such old-fashioned details as the timber mullion windows. In 1788 Philip called him back to design a new tower and a monument for Marchwiel church.

Much work was also done inside during the early 1770s, although again Philip was loath to get rid of anything old and interesting. In February 1771 he wrote to his steward John Caesar:

I would not have, upon Recollection, any Rummage yet made in the Lumber Room; among the many old, and strange things there. Perhaps somewhat on my view, may strike my convenience and therefore I wish nothing should be parted with from thence, till I have duly considered it.

Wyatt supplied new mahogany doors and tried to prevent the Hall and Drawing Room chimneys from smoking. (Philip had a dread of fire which can perhaps be traced back to 1751, when his cousin Charles Yorke had been almost killed in a blaze which also, and just as importantly to him, destroyed Lord Somers's famous collection of historical manuscripts.) The Hall and the new Drawing Room, created from the old Eating Parlour, received marble chimneypieces in the Neo-classical style, which were probably carved by John Devall the Younger, a craftsman much used by Wyatt. To complement them, 'Mr Rose the Plaisterer's men' put up Neo-classical plaster friezes in August–September 1773. Joseph Rose the Younger was another of Wyatt's favoured craftsmen, which suggests that he may have supervised the decoration of these rooms.

By the 1770s it had become unfashionable to have the bedrooms on the ground floor, so Meller's great bed was moved upstairs, and a new State Bedroom, hung with Chinese painted wallpaper, was created there to receive it. The Best Bedchamber became a dining-room and the Withdrawing Room was incorporated into an enlarged Saloon. In 1775 Philip's growing collection of books and manuscripts was brought down from the Study, in its rather remote position above the Chapel, to the Little Parlour, which was fitted up as the Library. The furniture that Philip had inherited from Meller and Hutton

was cherished, but new pieces were also bought from the London upholsterers Michael Thackthwaite, Edward France and John Cobb and the carver Thomas Fentham.

For the first time there was need for more than one bed in the nursery at Erddig. In eight and a half years Elizabeth gave birth to seven children; the two eldest, Simon and Etheldred, were painted together in a pastel portrait (now in the Chinese Room), which has a fine frame by Fentham. Then on Sunday 31 January 1779 Philip wrote in the family Bible:

This day at twenty minutes past one, to my irreparable Loss, and very just and great affliction, my most dear and honoured Wife, Elizabeth Yorke, departed this life, having nearly compleated her thirtieth year, being born on the 24th. of February 1748–9 (and married to me, the 2^{d} July 1770: On the Sunday fortnight preceding her death, She was brought to bed of a

The Chinese painted wallpaper was put up in the State Bedroom in the 1770s during the Yorkes' redecoration of the house

Daughter, between one and two months before her expected time, and the Fever which followed her *delivery* (in *itself* very dangerous & critical) left us in a few days, little hopes of her Recovery. Under the strongest Impression of her End, She supported herself (without complaints) with the greatest Composure, and strength of Mind, and with surprising Recollection as to all such things, as became the awfulness of that Time, and occasion; for in the beginning, and towards the conclusion of that fatal illness, she was free from Delirium.

He submitted himself to God 'with all humility and Resignation, and in his good and appointed time to be added to *those* ashes, wherewith my first Love and worldly affection, is buried.' With his usual thoroughness, he gave detailed instructions to John Caesar for her funeral: the oak coffin, covered in black cloth and fitted with black coffin furniture, a small engraved silver plate and no 'Glaring Ornaments', was to be laid in the family vault at Marchwiel; a funerary hatchment was to be hung from the Gallery window. That Christmas must have been a bleak one at Erddig, but Philip still found time to buy 'Dolls for my little Girls'. In 1782 he married Diana Meyrick, a widow who bore him a further six children and with whom he grew old more or less happily.

Philip Yorke was MP for Helston in Cornwall and then for the Cust pocket borough of Grantham, but he never spoke in the Commons, disliked going to London and was not much interested in national politics. As he wrote to his cousin Lord Hardwicke about the American war in 1775: 'I do assure your Lordship this most unnatural and bloody contention in America makes me quite sick at heart. A continental war seems to me preposterous and impractical.' Like his father, he was much happier being a country gentleman – organising the Denbighshire militia and serving as High Sheriff in 1786. His real passions were good talk, historical research and his park and estate (see Chapters Seven and Eight), around which he rode somewhat uncertainly. His neighbour, Charles 'Nimrod' Apperley, called him 'the worst horseman I ever saw in a saddle'. Philip had been elected a Fellow of the Society of Antiquaries at the early age of 24, and much of his later life was spent in his Library

absorbed in abstruse genealogical scholarship. In 1784 the old billiard-room in the basement became the Tribes Room, embellished with the coats of arms of the ancient ruling families of Wales. The culmination of his research was *The Royal Tribes of Wales*, published in two handsome folio volumes in 1799.

Philip was interested not only in the histories of the famous. He began the Erddig tradition of having the house and estate servants painted, and added verses describing their lives which he was honest enough to call '*Crude-ditties*'. Typical is that for the portrait of the housemaid Jane Ebbrell, painted by John Walters of Denbigh in 1793, when she was 87:

To dignifie our Servants' Hall
Here comes the Mother, of us all;
For seventy years, or near have passed her,
Since spider-brusher to the *Master*;
When busied then, from room to room,
She drove the dust, with brush, and broom
And by the virtues of her mop
To all uncleanness, put a stop:
But changing her *housemaiden* state,
She took our coachman, for a mate;
To whom she prov'd an useful gip,
And brought us forth a second whip:
Moreover, this, oft, when she spoke,
Her tongue, was midwife, to a joke,
And making many an happy *hit*,
Stands here recorded for a wit:
O! may she, yet some years, survive,
And breed her Grandchildren to *drive*!

The Custs' local poet, William Henry Chambers, composed verse of more conventional eulogy on the death of Philip Yorke in 1804 at the age of 61, after suffering 'with spasms on his chest':

When rich men die, who living claim'd respect
From riches only, on the scutcheon'd hearse
In awful grandeur waves each sable plume,
And pomp supplies the place of true regret;
But, when the man of worth exchanges life
For bliss eternal, how comfortless th' expanse
He seems to leave behind! Nor Passing-bell
Nor Rites-Funereal our attention claim;
But every thought to one emotion yields,
Sorrow awhile envelopes us around
And un-availing anguish reigns supreme.

Jane Ebbrell, Housemaid and Spider-brusher (b.1705/6); by John Walters, 1793 (Servants' Hall)

CHAPTER FOUR

THE NINETEENTH CENTURY

About Philip's successor, Simon Yorke II, 'There is not a great deal to say,' as the family historian, Albinia Cust, admitted. Indeed the same is true of all the four Simon Yorkes. (Like the kings of Denmark, the Yorke sons had a choice of only two names.) In character, he seems to have most resembled his amiable grandfather. Having been educated at Eton, he celebrated his coming-of-age at Erddig in 1792. The marble cistern now in the Dining Room was filled with punch, which was dispensed liberally. Charles Apperley (then fourteen) consumed so much that he had to be put to bed upstairs in a drunken stupor.

After Simon inherited Erddig in 1804, his stepmother moved back to her family home, Dyffryn

Simon Yorke II (1771–1834) and his sister Etheldred (1772–96); by Katherine Read, c.1775 (Chinese Room)

Aled, with her children, but he remained on good terms with his young halfbrothers and sisters, taking a friendly interest in their education and careers. In 1807 he sold the Newnham estate for reasons that his banker, Thomas Birch, explained: 'It will enable you to disencumber the Rest of your property, and I hope save a little money into the bargain, for it is always desirable to have some ready money, let a man's Property be ever so large.' In the same year he married Margaret Holland from Teyrdan near Abergele; a view of her home can be seen on the South Landing. They were to have six children, two of whom died in infancy. John Cust sent a Vulliamy bronze inkstand as a wedding present. Simon's halfbrothers and sisters clubbed together to buy the couple a huge Spode dinner service. As a friend who organised its delivery remarked, 'The Service you will soon receive is not for every day use: you will think it magnificent, and very ample as to quantity.' There had clearly been a major accident in the scullery, as Simon's aunt Anne Reynardson also offered day-to-day china. His halfbrother Piers sent a set of silver forks and a sideboard, and Simon himself ordered more plate from Rundells, the royal goldsmiths, in 1808. All these were put to use in the Dining Room, which his father had created from the Best Bedchamber.

Simon was a sociable man, who enjoyed visiting his numerous Cust and Yorke cousins in East Anglia and having them to stay at Erddig. The Dining Room must have been inadequate for his needs, as in 1826 he began the last major change made to the house. He removed Meller's dressing-room and closet to create a larger room and had it completely redecorated in Regency taste. The plasterers Vowells and Batty put up the deeply coffered plaster ceiling and frieze, and the yellow scagliola columns came from the London workshops of Browne & Co. The suite of 22 dining-chairs, made

Thomas Rogers, Carpenter (1781–1875), painted by William Jones in 1830 (Servants' Hall)

Simon Yorke III (1811–94), painted in 1835, the year after he inherited Erddig (Dining Room)

by Gillows of Lancaster, was a present from Margaret's brother John Holland. The room was designed by Thomas Hopper, who was already working in North Wales building the vast neo-Norman Penrhyn Castle in Caernarvonshire. That project was consuming all his energies, as he apologised to Simon Yorke in April 1829:

It has annoyed me very much that I have been so hard pressed for twice when I have been in Wales as it has prevented my having the pleasure of waiting on you. It would gratify me very truly to see you again although your work is done, but I hope & trust that if you think that I can be of any service you will command me. I fear I led you into more expense than you intended & I feel reluctant to make a charge but I know if I did not it would displease you and I will therefore say £35 but less would quite satisfy me. I paid £25 for the Chimney piece and whenever you have an opportunity of paying into Mess.rs Herries Farquhar and Co Bankers St James St as much less than £60 as you please you will oblige me but it is no matter how long times.

Simon Yorke clearly made good use of his new Dining Room, as in later life he was tormented with rheumatic gout. While the Dining Room was being modernised, work was also going on in the rest of the house. The Agent's Office and Housekeeper's Room received new fittings, the Still Room was wainscotted and paved, and the school room and bedroom were altered, perhaps because the last of their children was now away at school.

Albinia Cust remarked, quite rightly, 'The Squires of Erddig were not Art collectors in the strict meaning of the term.' However, like his father, Simon II cherished what they had, getting the paintings cleaned and varnished in 1820 and commissioning engravings of some of the earlier family portraits. In 1830 he also added to his father's series of portraits of the Erddig servants, writing explanatory verses in the same vein. Among those painted was the carpenter Thomas Rogers, who was to work at Erddig for 73 years. He had more reason than most to be so loyal, for in 1815 he had been seized by a press gang while repairing estate cottages at Plas Grono. He pleaded with his captors for a last chance to see his master before being sent to sea. As soon as Simon Yorke II discovered what had happened, he bought him out of naval service.

Although Simon Yorke III owned Erddig throughout almost the entire reign of Queen Victoria, he did even less to it than his father. With his grandfather's fear of fire, he ordered the blue glass bottles that can be seen in the Housekeeper's Room and hanging in the corridors. Fortunately, he never had to use these primitive early fire extinguishers. He also arranged the furniture in the Saloon more or less as we see it today, and had the steps up to it built in 1863.

In 1846 Simon III married one of his Cust cousins, Victoria, a daughter of Sir Edward Cust, the master of ceremonies in the royal household. Victoria Cust was a goddaughter of the Queen, who sent her a bracelet as a wedding present. The Queen's Golden Jubilee in 1887 was celebrated with a fête at Erddig. When the Queen made a royal tour of North Wales two years later, she was invited to visit the house, but preferred to stay near Llangollen. Victoria Yorke never got over the royal snub; in later life she referred to the Queen dismissively as 'Old Mother Bunch'. The Yorkes were content to live quietly at

Erddig, rarely leaving the house apart from holidays at the villa Victoria had bought in Barmouth. Simon III continued the family tradition of writing bad verse, which was mocked by his wife. He wrote to their son Philip in 1894: 'I am quite convinced that your mother loves me dearly – but hath a rather curious way of showing it, in regard to my rhyming propensities.' Paintings gave way to photographs of the servants, who were commemorated in uniformly optimistic terms. Simon III also commissioned more traditional memorials, like the funerary hatchments to the butlers John Davies and George Dickinson that now hang in the Servants' Hall.

The Yorkes' preservationist instinct was also inherited by Simon III's younger brother John. He had commanded the Royal Dragoons in the Crimean War and been severely wounded during the Charge of the Heavy Brigade at Balaclava in 1854. He kept the shrapnel splinters removed from his leg in a snuff-box. In 1876 he bought Plas Newydd, the home of the 'Ladies of Llangollen', Eleanor Butler and Sarah Ponsonby, and devoted the rest of his life to preserving it. In 1778 'the two

most celebrated virgins in Europe' had eloped from their repressive families and set up home together at Plas Newydd. Here they lived for the next 50 years, reading, writing and gossiping, sketching, embroidering and filling the house with all manner of curiosities. It became a popular destination for the growing number of visitors to North Wales in the early nineteenth century. Wordsworth came in 1824 and wrote of:

Sisters in love, a love allowed to climb
Even on this earth, above the reach of time!

As a boy General Yorke had known the Ladies, who had stuffed his pockets full of oranges when he had been thrown from his pony. He set about turning the house into a museum in their memory, but also imported further exhibits, added new wings, and fitted up oak battens to give the façade a suitably quaint neo-Elizabethan appearance. In 1877 his sister-in-law sent over box, magnolia, pampas grass and fig trees from Erddig for the garden; he in turn gave her the gates at the end of the Moss Walk. Thanks to his efforts, Plas Newydd survived, and is now owned by Glyndŵr District Council.

The Chinese Room and Conservatory in the late nineteenth century

CHAPTER FIVE
THE TWENTIETH CENTURY

As a child Philip Yorke II caught butterflies in the garden, which the butler George Dickinson helped him chloroform and mount for the family museum – a diverse assortment of curiosities, from an Indian bus ticket to a swordfish blade and a Zulu assegai. (Philip's younger brother Victor was to die in the first Boer War of 1881.) Philip did not get on with his father, who seems to have bullied him into marrying Annette Puleston in 1877. The marriage was a disaster from the start: Philip spent their honeymoon painting watercolours, and Annette left him shortly afterwards without a word, having apparently begged a lift on a milk float. He explained what had happened to a friend:

I write in bitter grief to you to tell you that I know nothing of her. She left me a fortnight ago, while we were staying with some friends of mine, the Humberstones of Glan-y-Wern.

She went off with her maid without ever wishing me Adieu or any one else in the house. Since then I have heard nothing of her, beyond that her maid came over to Erddig to ask for her things. I, not unnaturally, refused to see the hateful creature (who, I believe, is the cause of my wife's estrangement from me), and as no note came with her, I know nothing more of her, and I must look forward to a lifelong misery and loneliness, as I am doing now.

Years later they met by chance in the street: 'Is it peace, Philip?' 'Madam, let me show you to your carriage.' They never spoke again.

Philip spent the next 20 years touring Europe and the Holy Land, painting, writing and taking photographs. He returned, not to Erddig, but to London, where he worked among the poor of the East End. The stigma of his separation excluded him from much of Denbighshire society, but seems to have drawn him closer to his servants, whose welfare became his overriding concern.

Annette died in 1899, and Philip was at last free to begin a new life. He shared the contemporary passion for cycling, riding over 60 miles in a day even in his fifties. He found a soulmate in another keen cyclist, Louisa Scott, the daughter of a Wiltshire vicar. After a tea-party at Erddig in the summer of 1899, to which the local children were invited, she wrote in her diary: 'Mr Yorke is a paragon of goodness. Each child had a present as well as a good tea, games, boats etc.' Then by the flickering light of oil lamps they stood in the Entrance Hall reciting J. F. Edisbury's 'To the Cyclist':

If you want to know how to cure *real* rheumatic
Please listen to what I am going to sing –
Just buy a bicycle – with tyres pneumatic
And – with very slight practice – you'll find it *the*
    thing.

Louisa returned to Erddig several times, until in February 1902 she wrote in her diary:

13th February. We had a delightful drive & Mr. Yorke was most polite . . .
14th February. (St Valentine's Day). One of the happiest days of my life. Mr Yorke & I walked to Wrexham and coming home he said such pretty things to me & called me his 'sister'. . . . In the evening we learned Palmistry & at 12.15, under the picture of the former Philip Yorke (by Gainsborough) he asked me to become his wife. It seems a dream. I can hardly believe it is true.
15th February. The sense of my coming duties & responsibilities almost frighten me, but I have Philip to help me in my difficulties.

One of these responsibilities was to find a satisfactory housekeeper. This proved far from easy. Indeed, one housekeeper, Ellen Penketh, was taken to court for falsifying the household accounts. Although the judge instructed the jury to convict, they sided with Mrs Penketh and acquitted her. For

Philip II, Louisa and Simon IV Yorke sketching in the garden around 1908

once the sunny tone of Philip's verse disappeared, when he praised her successor, Miss Brown:

Her coming we may here remark
Brought to a close a period dark,
For long on us did Fortune frown
Until we welcomed good Miss Brown,
One whom this latter did replace
Did for five years our substance waste,
As foul a thief as e'er we saw,
Tho' white-washed by Un-Civil Law.

Success is said to spoil people; in reality, more are spoilt by failure, as the unhappy life of Simon Yorke IV illustrates. It all began so well, with general celebration on the estate in 1903, when the 54-year-old Philip II at last produced a male heir. A brother, Philip III, arrived two years later. Their father was determined that his children should enjoy the happy childhood he had been denied, and this they had, although he was old enough to be their grandfather. Simon was sent to Cheltenham College, but had to be withdrawn when his work proved not up to standard. He only managed to get into his great-great-grandfather's Cambridge college, Corpus, at the sixth attempt, and was then obliged to settle for an Ordinary rather than an Honours degree. He turned to rowing, but even here was surpassed by his brother.

Simon Yorke belonged to the generation just too young to have fought in the First World War. When his father died in 1922, he was still only nineteen, and the running of the estate was left to his mother until he came of age two years later. She organised a grand party at Erddig for the occasion. Group photographs of the family and servants were taken on the garden steps, but these images of a large and comfortable community are misleading. The size of the household staff had shrunk radically

The Yorke family in 1918: Philip II and Louisa flanked by their sons, Simon IV (left) and Philip III

during the war and never returned to its former level; many of those photographed had been hired only for the day. By the mid-1920s, the estate was in serious financial trouble, but Simon's only response was indignant bluster:

I hope something will be done about my cash at or before the Trustee Meeting. It is a perfect disgrace not having been able to get my £500 when it was due last November. I wonder how they think I am going to live here – I hear we were overdrawn £1000 before last Rent Day; a pretty good start!

At this key moment, when he desperately needed professional advice, he parted company with the agent who looked after most of the estate. The staff became increasingly reluctant to work for meagre wages in an uncomfortable and dilapidated house. Five left in one day in April 1927: Mrs Yorke suspected a 'Bolshevik plot'. Like Dorothy Yorke in the 1760s, she hoped for 'happy marriages for the boys to ladies with some money'. But neither of them was the marrying kind, and she became in-

creasingly alarmed by Simon's 'desultory and slack ways'.

During the 1930s the estate disintegrated rapidly, and the coming of the Second World War, the nadir of so many country houses, only made matters worse. Simon went into the army, but proved a hopeless soldier, at one point managing to loose a steam-roller that had been left in his charge. Life at Erddig in the austere post-war world was no better. The greatest danger was the nationalisation of the coal industry in 1947. Coal had supported the estate since the eighteenth century; now it threatened to undermine it, quite literally. Officials from the National Coal Board announced that Bersham colliery intended to drive shafts directly under the house. Simon protested, but to no avail. The south wing began to sink, cracks appeared in the walls, water poured through the leaking roofs on to the State Bed, and wet rot became rampant. Simon refused even to accept government compensation, 'as much of government money has been subscribed by people worse off than himself'. During the 1940s and '50s the staff shrank to two, and only the housekeeper, Mrs Lloyd, lived in. Simon became a recluse, leaving the house only to attend scout meetings or to go cubbing, his pockets stuffed with ginger biscuits. Visitors were not welcome, even in the grounds, where battered notices announced that all wheeled vehicles were prohibited. One by one, he cut his links with the outside world. The telephone installed by his father was removed. When the postman complained about being bitten by his dog, Simon simply stopped accepting deliveries to the house. There was no electricity.

Simon seems to have been fatalistic about the house and the garden, concentrating his efforts on buying up outlying pieces of land to consolidate the estate. The early eighteenth-century furniture was becoming increasingly valuable and was in desperate need of attention, but like a true Yorke he refused to part with any of it. Although Erddig might seem to be in terminal decline, at least it was still intact. He died in 1966, leaving no will.

Simon's younger brother, Philip III, inherited at the age of 61. He had already had one heart attack, and the sensible response would have been to sell up and live in comfortable retirement on the proceeds. But Philip Yorke was never much interested in comfort or common sense. His years as the last squire of Erddig were to prove a triumphant and appropriately bizarre climax to a full and varied life. After graduating from Cambridge in 1927, he studied for the priesthood at Ridley Hall, but his unorthodox interpretation of scripture did not go down well with his teachers. He dismissed Solomon, epitome of biblical wisdom, as 'one of the most brainless men in all history'. It was suggested that he find another career. Like the first Philip Yorke, he loved the theatre, and in November 1930 he joined the Northampton Repertory Company, which included such future West End stars as Max Adrian and James Hayter. However, Philip's enthusiasm could not disguise his inability to act. He turned to stage management, founding the Country Theatre Players, who toured plays by Somerset Maugham and Ben Travers round Kent and Sussex in a second-hand bus. The house may not always have been full, but the notices were complimentary:

Mr Yorke won almost overnight popularity in Bexhill – on stage and off. He was not always word-perfect on Fridays, let alone on Mondays, a circumstance that tended to keep the rest of the company on the hop. But

Philip Yorke III on the roof of his Utility Tours bus in the 1950s

the swish of the waves under the Pavilion floor was good cover for the prompter.

After war service, he toured Europe by car and bicycle, returning frequently to Spain, of which he was particularly fond. Between trips there was a bewildering succession of jobs – prep. school teacher, security guard, groundsman, tour operator. In 1953 he founded Utility Tours to take holiday-makers round France and Spain in a grey dormobile christened 'Tilly', which he drove himself. The regime was fairly spartan for all; as the brochure pointed out encouragingly, 'The management sleeps in the bus'. Unable to compete with the rise of the big package holiday companies, he decided to join them, becoming a courier for Horizon. Book-keeping was never his strong point:

The invoice book which you have sent for paying the bills is perfectly ridiculous. It is filled with a con-glomeration of unnecessary details in ridiculous lan-guages and is absurdly unwieldy. Fortunately I have my musical saw with me and I have been able to cut the book in two. This is the best kind of economy as nobody loses by it, and the other half will do for whoever is ass enough to take on the job of working under your so-called management next year. Unfor-tunately I have not made the cut very straight as I think the saw wants sharpening.

Philip's musical saw (now in the Tribes Room) and euphonium were popular turns at fêtes in the Wrexham area, where he also enjoyed demonstrat-ing his skill on the penny-farthing. His theatrical training came in useful for the lantern slide lectures he gave about his travels in Spain. When he became squire of Erddig, he was asked increasingly to lecture on the house and its history.

It would be easy to pigeon-hole Philip Yorke as an eccentric, but in fact his previous careers turned out to be a surprisingly useful preparation for life at Erddig. He had a gift for improvisation; unlike his brother, he was gregarious; and his worldly needs were 'about on the level of those of an unemployed oyster', as he put it. At night, he camped out in the freezing, collapsing house, having booby-trapped the doors with Heath Robinson burglar alarms made from empty evaporated milk tins, string and bamboo. Calor gas lamps, rigged up in front of eighteenth-century silver salvers, provided the only

light. During the day, the house was once again full of people, who gathered for huge vegetarian meals in the Servants' Hall. Helpers were drafted in from the neighbourhood to begin makeshift repairs: local boys could earn a penny a bar for painting the gates. The Coal Board shored up the worst of the subsidence and the National Trust also started to show an interest.

Philip Yorke was determined to save 'this unique establishment for which my family have foregone many luxuries and comforts over seven gener-ations'; so was the Trust. It should have been straightforward; it was not. The negotiations were to last six and a half years. Philip was instinctively suspicious of all officialdom, and the National Trust became entangled in his mind with the Treasury to such an extent that he took to muttering angrily about the 'National Distrust'.

Gradually, the obstacles were overcome. In 1970 the Trust calculated that £800,000 was needed to provide a proper endowment for Erddig. This seemed an impossibly large sum to find until the property boom of the early 1970s transformed the calculations. Selling a small parcel of land for building raised £1 million; the NCB also agreed to pay £120,000 compensation and to stop mining under the house. The State Bed was removed to the Victoria & Albert Museum for urgently needed conservation, but Philip was insistent that Erddig's great collection of furniture should not be separ-ated from the house. Throughout February 1973 two of the Trust's historic buildings staff, Merlin Waterson and Gervase Jackson-Stops, sat in the frigid Dining Room systematically sorting through the huge archive of family papers, which yielded a succession of exciting discoveries. Their efforts seem finally to have convinced Philip that the Trust was in earnest, as he signed the handover documents the following month.

Shortly afterwards, he was standing on the steps outside the Entrance Hall in the late afternoon sun, when he turned and said to a friend: 'It's probably what my father would have liked – the old place restored to its former glory.' And so – after a great deal of further work by researchers, architects, builders, conservators and gardeners and numerous enthusiastic volunteers – it has been.

An upstairs passage in the early 1970s. Most of the house was by then in this state

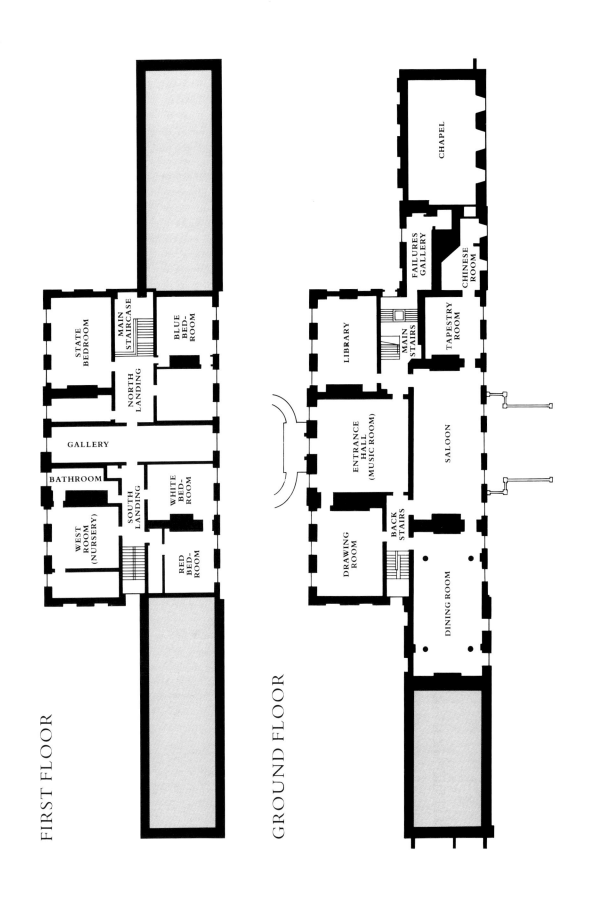

FIRST FLOOR

STATE
BEDROOM

MAIN
STAIRCASE

BLUE
BED-
ROOM

NORTH
LANDING

GALLERY

BATHROOM

SOUTH
LANDING

WHITE
BED-
ROOM

WEST
ROOM
(NURSERY)

RED
BED-
ROOM

GROUND FLOOR

CHAPEL

FAILURES
GALLERY

CHINESE
ROOM

LIBRARY

MAIN
STAIRS

TAPESTRY
ROOM

ENTRANCE
HALL
(MUSIC ROOM)

SALOON

DRAWING
ROOM

BACK
STAIRS

DINING ROOM

LOWER GROUND FLOOR

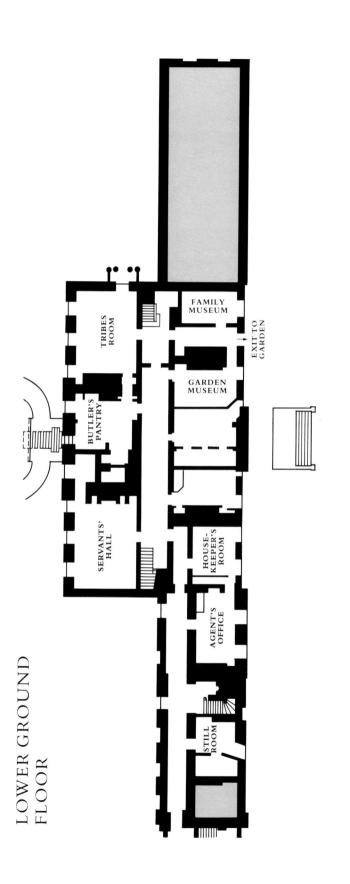

TRIBES ROOM

FAMILY MUSEUM

EXIT TO GARDEN

GARDEN MUSEUM

BUTLER'S PANTRY

SERVANTS' HALL

HOUSE-KEEPER'S ROOM

AGENT'S OFFICE

STILL ROOM

N

Only the rooms named are open to the public

PLANS OF THE HOUSE

CHAPTER SIX

TOUR OF THE OUTBUILDINGS AND HOUSE

The tour of Erddig begins with the domestic offices – buildings designed to meet the needs of house, garden, park and estate. Visitors are shown these areas first, because the social history of Erddig, and the lives of the various staff who worked here, are recorded with a detail matched by few country houses.

THE JOINER'S SHOP

The Joiner's Shop and other workshops in this area date from the nineteenth century, although in the eighteenth century the Joiner's and Carpenter's Shops and the sawpit were sited nearer the house, in what was later to become the Outer Stableyard.

During the last quarter of the nineteenth century the house carpenter, John Jones, and an estate foreman, William Gittins, worked alongside each other in this workshop, with two apprentices. The workshop is still used today as a joiner's shop.

Each carpenter owned his own set of tools, which were carefully stored in a box and never left lying around when not in use. The two-man sawpit outside provided handsawn timber until the latter part of the nineteenth century, when it was replaced by the steam-driven sawmill.

Erddig carpenters were involved in a wide variety of work; more intricate work, such as repairs to

furniture, was generally the responsibility of the joiner. Several were recorded in paintings or photographs and celebrated in verse. John Walters's portrait of Edward Prince of 1792 includes a scroll inscribed with witty verse composed by Philip Yorke I and shows a carpenter who had served the family since his teens. A portrait of Prince's successor, Thomas Rogers, commissioned by Simon Yorke II in 1830, also incorporates verse composed by his employer. Both portraits are on show in the Servants' Hall (illustrated on p.21).

THE ESTATE YARD

The workshops and stores in this area were rebuilt in the early nineteenth century for the use of the estate foreman and his staff of 30. The staff were responsible for repairs to the farmhouses and cottages, roads and bridges, fences and footpaths on the 1,800 or so acres of the estate, including parkland. The yard continues to function in the same way and is now used by National Trust estate staff.

THE SAWPIT

Timber from the estate was first seasoned by being stored for a time in the lean-tos around the yard. Until the end of the nineteenth century, when a steam-powered sawmill was introduced, the timber was then reduced to manageable widths in the two-man sawpit, before being stored again for further seasoning. The blade of the 'top and bottom saw' would be regularly lubricated from a grease pot kept in a recess in the wall. Saws hang on the wall.

THE BLACKSMITH'S SHOP

There was probably not a blacksmith's shop here until the first quarter of the nineteenth century, as one does not appear on a plan of the estate yard of about 1800.

In the eighteenth century most decorative ironwork supplied to Erddig was made by Robert

Davies of Croesfoel, near Wrexham. This included a magnificent pair of wrought-iron gates and screens which were set up on the west front of the house in the 1720s, but swept away in the remodelling of the 1770s.

By 1790, however, the accounts record that William Williams worked regularly for the estate, although he appears not to have been an employee. Like the carpenters, he is celebrated in a portrait of 1793 by John Walters, on show in the Servants' Hall. Williams was responsible for the iron railings on the west front entrance, but successive blacksmiths were involved in a variety of both utilitarian and decorative ironwork. These ranged from everyday ironmongery for the estate, such as latches and hinges, the repairing of farm tools and shoeing of horses, as well as making the lead cast shells for the garden fountains. The set of early eighteenth-century garden gates bought from nearby Stansty Park by Philip Yorke II in 1908 was repaired by his smith Joseph Wright and set up by the National Trust in the 1970s as a *clairvoyée* at the far end of the canal.

(Left) The Joiner's Shop in 1973 before restoration

(Right) Alan Knight restoring the Stansty gates in the Blacksmith's Shop in the 1970s

THE WAGON SHED

The timber wagon was used regularly to transport trees extracted from the estate woodlands. The vehicle could serve as a two-wheeled timber carriage for use on rough ground and dense woodland, or it could be extended to form a four-wheeled vehicle capable of carrying a full-length tree trunk. The wheelwrighting of the front bob dates it to the mid-nineteenth century, whilst the rear bob is of about 1900.

The 'dray', or lorry, of the same date was used principally at harvest time.

THE LIME YARD AND SAWMILL

This is approached through the Dog Yard where several lapping pools are incorporated into the stone gutter. A plan of 1800 names the rooms off it as 'Flesh Yard', 'Kenel' and 'Dog Kitchen'.

The Lime Yard's curved retaining wall allowed a horse and loaded cart to turn without difficulty. The large cast-iron mortar mill was acquired in the early 1900s and used by the estate foreman and his staff. In it lime was mixed with sand and ash to provide mortars which were used on the estate buildings and for jobs such as the addition of Dutch gables to the garden pavilions in 1912.

The block mould was used during the 1900s for casting concrete blocks for new buildings, an example of the estate's self-sufficiency.

The sawmill was converted from a former hogsty and stable, and the machinery was the responsibility of Thomas Roberts, sawyer and engineer for 49 years.

The steam boiler (the present one was bought second-hand in 1935) powered both the sawmill and the mortar mill, and also ground corn. It was the unenviable job of the youngest of the estate staff to descale the inside of the boiler: this once resulted in William Gittins becoming wedged upside-down in the manhole. The boiler had a new lease of life in the late 1940s and '50s, when Simon Yorke IV's disagreements with the Coal Board about mining beneath the estate, led him to forbid the burning of anything but wood in the house. The boiler itself, however, continued to be fed by coal.

In the other half of the sawmill building is an exhibition and video presentation describing the National Trust's work in restoring Erddig.

THE OUTER YARD

The central brick-built midden was originally heaped with straw and dung from the stables. The long arched hay barn is now occupied by the tearoom and shop.

CARTS

There are two dung carts: a tumbrel of about 1910 made by Crosskills of Beverley, and a tipping dung cart of about 1880–1900.

THE STABLEYARD

The Outer Yard, the Stableyard and the Laundry beyond form part of a new service wing built on the south side of the house by Philip Yorke I between 1772 and 1774. This replaced the two service wings of the 1720s which flanked the forecourt of the west front. The architect James Wyatt (1746–1813) was probably responsible for establishing the general plan, with William Turner of Whitchurch and others specifying the detail and executing the scheme. The original approach for horses and carriages would have been via the rusticated archway, with its keystone dated 1774, leading off the drive to the west front entrance. Inside, the original stalls and mangers are set behind Tuscan columns.

The Yorke's attitude to their liveried staff was informal: Philip Yorke I was concerned only with the honesty and reliability of his grooms and coachmen. He provided them with serviceable, rather than extravagant, livery and rejected the more ostentatious display of the higher aristocracy. Philip Yorke I himself was considered by his neighbour, Charles Apperley, to be a figure of fun on horseback – dressed as he was in a blue military cloak, silver spurs and cocked hat.

VEHICLES

IN CARRIAGE HOUSE:

The Skeleton Boot Victoria of about 1860 was intended for use during fine weather and constructed so as to be pulled by a single horse or pair. It is unusual therefore to find a folding, glazed screen in front of the hood frame, which allowed protection from the weather. The panels of the body are embellished with decoration imitating split cane.

Bicycles in the Carriage House

The float was used as a general purpose vehicle for carrying produce or stock. The original iron wheels have been replaced by rubber tyres.

The early twentieth-century Governess Cart, also known as the Tub Cart, has a door at the back and provided safe transport for children. These carts were generally pulled by small ponies.

IN SMALLER CARRIAGE HOUSE:

A 1907 Rover, bought in the 1920s from the chimney sweep, who had acquired it from the Rector of Marchwiel. It was Erddig's first car and was licensed until 1924.

The Austins are 1924 and 1927 models.

The bicycles include Philip Yorke II's nineteenth-century 'Bone Shaker' by J. Hill of Piccadilly and several earlier penny-farthings, most of which were acquired by Philip Yorke III; the first in his collection was bought for a shilling from a scrap-yard in Aberystwyth.

THE DAIRY

This room contains a photographic exhibition of the Yorkes' servants, with tape-recorded reminiscences of Philip Yorke III and retired staff, recollecting life at Erddig before the First World War.

THE LAUNDRY YARD

Meller's original laundry was swept away when Philip Yorke I demolished the range to the west of the house and replaced it by much more spacious accommodation. Grouped around the little enclosed yard are the Bakehouse, Laundry and Scullery. In the nineteenth century this area was entirely the domain of the female staff.

THE BAKEHOUSE

Bread is still baked here on a regular basis using the scuffle ovens, now converted to gas. These were originally heated for several hours with wooden faggots, the ashes were then raked or 'scuffled-out' on to the floor, and the dough slid in on long wooden peels.

IMPLEMENTS

They include a wooden dough chest and an eighteenth-century proving cupboard, as well as a selection of baker's peels and a baker's docker (a roller with metal spikes used for releasing unwanted air from the dough). Also on show are two early twentieth-century dough mixers.

35

THE WET AND DRY LAUNDRIES

The Laundry occupies two rooms: one used for washing, the other for drying and ironing. The former was supplied with hot water from two large coppers; the cold water came from a pump. Clothes and linen were washed, scrubbed and rinsed in the ceramic sinks, made in nearby Ruabon, while a vent in the high ceiling allowed the clouds of steam to escape. Here the laundry of both family and servants would have been undertaken on a weekly basis, the finest clothes being laundered by the best laundress.

One Erddig laundress, Alice Jones, was celebrated in verse by Philip Yorke II in 1912:

More than eight years her care has been
To keep our linen white and clean.
Bearing in patience, we might say,
The Burden and the heat of day.
And though, by duty at her post,
She is less often seen than most,
Her tuneful song in accents clear
Is heard within our Chapel here.

The Wet Laundry

WASHING IMPLEMENTS

These include a zinc dolly tub and wooden dolly, scrubbing boards, copper possers and an early manual washing-machine.

MANGLES

A hand-geared two-roller mangle and folding tabletop mangle – 'a topper' – were used to wring out wet clothes.

Throughout the eighteenth and nineteenth centuries there was a mangle in the Laundry. The box mangle now occupying the Dry Laundry was made by Baker of London and has an ingenious gearing device which allows the handle to be turned continuously in one direction while the box of stones trundles backwards and forwards.

DRYING AND IRONING

The cast-iron drying racks, running in and out on wheels, were installed in the mid-nineteenth century and were warmed from below by a small stove. Ironing was done on the benches under the windows using a variety of flat irons and special irons – 'goffering' irons or 'fluting' tongs being essential for ruffles and frills, 'glossing' irons to give sheens to collars, and 'tally' irons for made-up bows.

THE SCULLERY

Adjacent to the New Kitchen, this was used for the preparation of vegetables, fish and meat as well as the washing of dishes. Opposite the Scullery was the Meat Pantry with frames from which to hang hams and flitches of bacon.

THE NEW KITCHEN

Architecturally one of the grandest rooms at Erddig, the New Kitchen was built in the early 1770s and was originally completely detached from the rest of the house, due largely to Philip Yorke I's fear of fire. By the nineteenth century, however, a linking block had been built and the windows on the north wall were blocked in to form cupboards.

The room is dominated by the large Venetian window on the east side and three great rusticated arches on the south, the centre one housing the range, installed *c.*1900. Above two of the arches

*The Dry
Laundry*

the old adage 'Waste Not Want Not' is painted as a pertinent reminder to the staff of the need for thrift.

Accounts of the annual wages of Meller's staff show that in 1725 the cook was the highest paid, with a salary of £21 per year, over twice that of the housekeeper, although by the next century their relative status was to be reversed. The last time there was anything like a full complement of staff at Erddig was just before the First World War, when the housekeeper, Mrs Brown, had overall responsibility for the Kitchen with Mrs Gillam, the head gardener's wife, who did much of the cooking, assisted by three kitchen maids. Their task was made more complicated by the fact that many of the Yorkes, beginning with Philip I, were vegetarians.

KITCHEN EQUIPMENT

Many of the items on show, collected by the late Harry Best of Vivod, are typical of those listed in an inventory of kitchen equipment made in 1834, following the death of Simon Yorke II. They included a set of copper fish kettles, preserving pans, moulds, frying pans and stew pans, various buckets, bread tins, ice moulds, a spice bag, tea kettle and a marble mortar.

FURNITURE

The mahogany longcase clock with satinwood banding and beech panels was made by H. Lote of Wrexham in about 1830.

CERAMICS

ON DRESSER:

Local countryware pottery was made at Buckley, near Mold.

THE SERVANTS' PASSAGE

Situated above the linking block to the main house were the Housekeeper's Bedroom and Sitting Room with a window conveniently over the back door (on the right) from where she could lower a key to let in staff who had been allowed out in the evening.

The Servants' Passage forms part of the south wing added to the house by John Meller in the 1720s, though it was then an open arcade. Above

The New Kitchen

the passage were the 'day', 'night' and 'middle' nurseries used by the last Simon and Philip Yorke, the first room being decorated with a Kate Greenaway wallpaper.

PHOTOGRAPHS

The passage is lined with photographs of the Erddig staff, the earliest of which is a copy of a daguerreotype of 1852. Other group photographs were taken in 1887 and 1912, and all have accompanying doggerel verse composed by Philip Yorke II.

THE STILL-ROOM

Originally used to distil cordial waters for dinners, medicinal purposes and scents, the Still-Room was the domain of the housekeeper, where less perishable foodstuffs, such as tea, coffee, sugar and preserves were stored, many in the labelled drawers and cupboards. By the nineteenth century still-rooms were used for preparing light breakfasts and afternoon tea.

CERAMICS

An early nineteenth-century Derby dinner service, given to Philip Yorke II by his Aunt, Mrs Congreve, in 1892.

THE SERVANTS' PASSAGE

Hung outside the Still-Room is the 'Erddig Prayer', a reminder of Philip Yorke I's preoccupation with fire precautions. The mechanical bell-pull system above is mid-nineteenth-century.

Beyond and to the right is a short flight of stairs leading to the Servery, from where food was taken into the Dining Room. A dumb waiter, installed in the nineteenth century, assisted with the carrying of dishes.

THE AGENT'S OFFICE

Together with the adjacent Housekeeper's Room, the Agent's Office formed the administrative centre of the house and estate. The Agent was responsible for paying wages, keeping accounts and organising the work of the outdoor staff.

Both Edisbury and Meller were served by stew-

The 'Erddig Prayer' in the Servants' Passage

ards, the latter by Richard Jones, who managed Meller's affairs in Wales while his nephew, Simon Yorke I, assisted him in London. Jones oversaw the progress of alterations to the house and garden and managed relations with Erddig's neighbours.

John Caesar, Philip Yorke I's agent, performed similar duties, managing Erddig staff in his employer's absence. Caesar appraised him of William Emes's improvements to the park and was responsible for day-to-day matters, such as removing snow off the roof of the house. Caesar was succeeded by his son Jacky, who was less conscientious: in 1787 he was dismissed when it was discovered that he had been paying himself higher wages than he was due.

PICTURES, PLANS AND NOTICES

Family portraits, estate plans and notices are hung around the walls, including one issued by Philip Yorke II prohibiting the unauthorised removal of unripe fruit from the gardens.

FURNITURE

The fire-screen was given to Philip Yorke II in 1906 as a birthday present from his second wife, Louisa. The scene is a copy of a typical Victorian genre painting by S. E. Waller – *Alone*, exhibited at the Royal Academy in 1896. The frame was made by Brown's of Chester for £5.

The Agent's Office

ABOVE FIREPLACE:

*The giltwood mirror, c.*1800, incorporates a panel depicting the figure of Mars. Either side of it are 'rustic' corner cupboards with applied bamboo-style decoration.

ESTATE EQUIPMENT

A selection of surveying, measuring and weighing equipment, including a nineteenth-century measuring chain, a brass spirit-level, postal scales and a stick barometer.

Outside in the passage, Ordnance Survey maps of 1899 illustrate the extent of the Erddig estate.

THE HOUSEKEEPER'S ROOM

The Housekeeper's Room is strategically situated between the Still-Room, Kitchen and Scullery to the south and the Servants' Hall to the west. James Wyatt advised Philip Yorke I on the arrangement of these rooms when alterations were being made in the 1770s. In a letter to Philip Yorke he proposed that a door be opened from the existing house-keeper's room and old larder to give more space and provide a china store.

The housekeeper was in overall charge of all the female indoor staff, including the cook, and she presided over their daily routines of cleaning the house and preparing food. She was specifically responsible for the valuable china and linen and for ordering provisions which could not be provided from the estate. She also planned meals, particularly when guests were being entertained.

The Yorkes considered their housekeepers to be the linchpin of all domestic arrangements. Miss Brown, housekeeper to Philip Yorke II between 1907 and 1914, typically began her day by checking the cleaning of the downstairs rooms and the early morning laying of fires by the housemaids before the family rose. After breakfast and chapel, she met Mrs Yorke to agree the day's menu and to discuss any other household matters. The remainder of her time was spent ensuring the efficient running of the Kitchen, Scullery, Laundry, Bakehouse and the maids' work in the rest of the house. When the family was not in residence, the housekeeper supervised the protection of the valuable furniture and textiles.

In 1951 Simon Yorke IV employed a Bavarian housekeeper, Victoria Aschenbrenner, who was joined in 1953 by two other German girls, Hildegard 'Poppi' Stenherr and Evelyn Voigt. This explains the labels written in German on the shelves of the linen cupboard.

FIRE GRENADES

The blue Victorian bottles on the other shelves of the linen cupboard are fire grenades, the design of which was patented in 1883 by H.D. Harden of Chicago and which were sold by the Harden Star Hand Grenade Extinguisher Company. The bottles contained a mixture of water, salt and ammonium chloride. When thrown into the centre of a fire, the ammonium chloride was heated to boiling point and produced fumes which were supposed to blanket the fire. In practice, however, they were no more effective than plain water.

CARPET SWEEPER

The Witch Dust Extractor, with bellows covered in Brussels carpet, was manufactured in Birmingham *c.*1905.

FURNITURE

The room is furnished with largely eighteenth- and nineteenth-century pieces relegated from the family rooms.

PHOTOGRAPHS

LEFT OF FIREPLACE:

They include two taken on the occasion of Simon Yorke IV's coming-of-age in 1924.

THE SERVANTS' HALL

This room was used continuously as a servants' hall from 1720. An inventory of 1726, however, lists two halls: the 'New' and 'Old', of which this is certainly one, the other having been swept away in the alterations of the 1770s. The Yorkes did not appear to mind that the Servants' Hall looked out directly on to the main entrance. In the post-war period it became a kitchen, when the large New Kitchen was abandoned.

Philip Yorke III regularly entertained visitors here in the late 1960s and '70s with substantial teas of bread and jam.

PICTURES

The portraits of the house and estate servants are perhaps the most famous feature of Erddig. They comprise two sets, one painted by a local Wrexham artist, John Walters of Denbigh, between 1791 and 1793, the other by William Jones, dated 1830. The portrait of the black coachboy stands outside these groups. Philip Yorke I seems to have begun the tradition of painting the family servants in the 1790s, and he added most of the doggerel verses that describe their jobs and characters; these were published by him in his *Crude-ditties* (1802). The tradition was carried on through the nineteenth century by photographic groups (hung in the passage outside).

CLOCKWISE FROM RIGHT OF RANGE:

WILLIAM JONES, 1830
Thomas Rogers, Carpenter (1781–1875)
Dated 1830
The estate carpenter, who was 49 in 1830, worked at Erddig for 73 years.

Edward Barnes, Woodman (b.1761/2)
Dated 1830
When commissioning this picture, Simon Yorke II made his own crude sketch of what he wanted.

The Housekeeper's Room

*Thomas Jones,
Butcher and
Publican
(b.1759/60); by
John Walters, 1796
(Servants' Hall)*

JOHN WALTERS of Denbigh
Mrs Jane Ebbrell, Housemaid and Spider-brusher
(b.1705/6)
Dated 1793
Seated outside her cottage, with her broom and
mop beside her, at the age of 87. She had worked for
John Meller, then married Simon Yorke I's coachman. Their son was in turn coachman to Simon's
son Philip Yorke I.

Jack Henshaw, Gamekeeper (b.1731/2)
Dated 1791
Painted at the age of 59. The house in the back-
ground is Dyffryn Aled, the home of Philip Yorke
I's second wife, Diana Meyrick.

Jack Nicholas, Kitchen Man (b.1719/20)
Dated 1791
Painted at the age of 71.

William Williams, Blacksmith (b.1722/3)
Dated 1793
Painted at the age of 70.

Thomas Jones, Butcher and Publican (b.1759/60)
Dated 1796
Painted at the age of 36. This is the only picture in
the series not to represent a direct employee on the
estate. According to the published version of the
verse inscription, he kept 'a Butcher's Stall, and the
Royal Oak Public-house, at Wrexham'.

Edward Prince, Carpenter (b.1718/19)
Signed and dated 1792
Painted at the age of 73. Erddig appears in the
background. His father, Charles Prince, was carpenter at Erddig in the time of John Meller, and a John
Prince worked as carpenter to Joshua Edisbury from
about 1690.

WILLIAM JONES, 1830
Thomas Pritchard, Gardener (b.1762/3)
Dated 1830
Painted at the age of 67.

BRITISH, late eighteenth-century
Formerly called 'John Meller's Coachboy'
This was previously thought to be the first of the
Erddig servant portraits, to which Philip Yorke I
had added his verses later in the eighteenth century.
However, it is now clear that the portrait itself is
also late eighteenth-century, and it has recently
been revealed by infra-red photography to have
had an inscription painted out giving the sitter's
name – John Hanby – and age – 25, but no date. The
picture was probably acquired and the inscription
hidden so it could serve as a portrait to commem-
orate Meller's horn-playing servant.

*'John Meller's Coachboy'; painted in the late eighteenth
century (Servants' Hall)*

The mahogany longcase clock has an early eighteenth-
century case, while the mechanism itself, signed by
Edmund Appley, Charing Cross, is earlier.

The black jacks were used to serve beer from the
nearby Brew-House. Servants were provided with
a weekly allowance of beer as an alternative to
unsafe drinking water.

HATCHMENTS

Hatchments are lozenge-shaped boards usually
painted with the coat of arms of the late owner and
traditionally hung above the entrance of his house.
It is characteristic of Erddig that two of its butlers,
John Davies and George Dickinson, are remem-
bered here in this form. Dickinson was particularly
popular with Simon Yorke III's children, helping
them to catch, chloroform and mount butterflies to
exhibit in the family museum. He died at Erddig
whilst under chloroform himself during a minor
operation.

SWORDS AND AXES

ON CEILING:

Each of the 68 radiating swords of the Denbighshire
Militia is engraved with a number and the image of
a fox. The Militia was founded in May 1760, the
Yorkes holding officer rank: Philip Yorke I was
commissioned as captain in 1778 and many of the
staff served in the regiment.

The fire axes are another reminder of the Yorke's
fear of fire.

FURNITURE

The room is simply furnished with pieces of
seventeenth- and eighteenth-century country furniture. The oak refectory table is surrounded by
seventeenth-century oak stools and eighteenth-century chairs. The highback settle is also eighteenth-
century.

THE BUTLER'S PANTRY

The Butler's Pantry has occupied this room since
the house was built. The door in the corner leads
down to the cellar and from this room the butler
was able to gain easy access to the front entrance to
allow visitors into the house. The butler was the
senior member of the male staff and was responsible
for the footmen, two of whose liveries are displayed
in the far cupboard. However, in the early eighteenth century, Meller's accounts show that his
butler, John Jones, was paid only £10 per year,
almost half that paid to the cook. By the mid-
eighteenth century Philip Yorke I's butler, Thomas
Newcome, was paid £25 and in 1903 Philip Yorke

Footmen's liveries in the Butler's Pantry

II's butler, Mr Wooton, received a modest salary of £55 per year.

The butler had a number of duties apart from managing the cellar. He was responsible for the family silver and however late a dinner might go on, the butler had to ensure that the silver was washed, polished and put away in the Strong Room before he or the footman could go to bed; the latter usually slept in a small bed in front of the safe door itself. The butler also supervised the washing of the finest china and glass in the lead-lined sink.

CONTENTS

Many of the items are similar to those found in the Butler's Pantry of John Meller's household in 1726:

A knife box, sub-divided into two sections.

A hardwood butler's tray on folding stand.

A Harrods knife cleaner with cast-iron frame.

An oval papier mâché bowl, used for washing glasses.

A wicker basket with paraffin primer stove, teapot, cups and plates, *c.*1903.

Three 'New Snapshot' mousetraps, patented 1894 and made at Johnstone, Glasgow.

A selection of assorted wine glasses, decanters and soda siphons.

SILVER

ON LEFT:

Two of the pantry cupboards have been adapted to display some of the finest pieces from the collection, including plate inherited from the Hutton branch of the family.

The mid-eighteenth-century soup tureen and cover on lion mask and paw feet was made in 1750 by Paul Crespin (1694–1770), one of the great Rococo silversmiths.

The bell-shaped jugs, engraved with the Hutton arms, are by Edward Vincent, 1736.

The bell-shaped tankard with double-scroll handle and gadrooned rim and foot is engraved with borders of vines, barley ears and bacchanalian masks as well as the Hutton arms. It was made by Jacob Marsh in 1768.

The silver-mounted gourd goblet was made *c.*1725, the Hutton, Yorke and Cust arms added *c.*1770.

The four sauce boats by Walter Brind are engraved with the Yorke and Cust arms.

The spherical soap dish dates from about 1740.

The sugar caster is by Simon Pantin, 1715.

One of a pair of 17th-century silver sconces.

Two mahogany tea caddies, one containing tea canisters and a sugar canister by John Jacob of 1739, and the other with a covered sugar bowl of about 1740 by Edward Feline, with two earlier eighteenth-century tea canisters by Simon Pantin.

The silver salvers on lion paw feet and key pattern brackets engraved with the arms of Yorke, Meller and Hutton are early nineteenth-century.

A silver cake basket pierced and engraved with the arms of Hutton, Yorke and Cust by Peter Archambo, 1734.

The three coffee pots are mid-eighteenth-century. The less heavily decorated one was presented by the Erddig servants to Philip Yorke II on his marriage to his first wife Annette Puleston in 1877.

The Dining Room

THE DINING ROOM

This room was formed from the Best Bedchamber of Edisbury's late seventeenth-century house, which Meller then enlarged in the 1720s by the addition of a dressing-room and closet. The Best Bedchamber became a dining-room at the end of the eighteenth century, when Philip Yorke I moved the State Bed to the first floor. It was further altered and enlarged in 1826–7, when the architect Thomas Hopper was commissioned by Simon Yorke II to remodel the room in a Neo-classical style.

Simon Yorke was probably introduced to Hopper through the latter's work at Penrhyn Castle, near Bangor, a neo-Norman castle begun in the 1820s (also now the property of the National Trust).

At Erddig, Hopper chose a Graeco-Roman style, combining a Roman Doric order for the columns and pilasters with a Greek coffered ceiling. Hollow scagliola columns and pilasters were supplied by Joseph Browne & Co. of London for £148 19s. They appear to support the load-bearing beams, inserted in place of the original partitions, and divide the room into three pleasing compartments: a vestibule area to the north (near end) and at the south a serving area leading from the Servery.

The plasterwork was executed by Vowells and Batty, who were presumably London craftsmen, to judge by their large travelling expenses. Hopper obtained the carved white Siena marble chimney-piece for £25; he also altered the flues so that the new fireplace could be sited on the west wall.

The present colour scheme of green and white echoes Hopper's original, although it dates from the restoration of the house between 1974 and 1977.

Anna Jemima Yorke (1754–70), possibly painted posthumously by William Hoare of Bath (Dining Room)

TABLE SETTING

The table is usually laid either for dinner or for dessert, echoing a view of the room in an Edwardian photograph and based on Mrs Beeton's *Book of Household Management*. The damask table-cloth, with Egyptian motifs of acanthus, lotus, lions and sphinxes, dates from about 1830.

The Indian Tree dinner service was originally bought as a wedding present for Simon Yorke II and his new wife Margaret Holland in 1807.

The dessert service is Spode, *c*.1820. Each of the 24 pieces is painted with a named British bird on a blue ground.

The pair of three-light silver candelabra, 1798, was made by William Frisbie. The candles themselves are surmounted by self-descending shade holders.

PICTURES

FROM TOP LEFT OF FAR, SOUTH WALL:

? EDWARD WRIGHT (active 1730s)
Simon Yorke I (1696–1767)
The first of the Yorkes of Erddig. Painted around the time he inherited the estate, in 1733, from his uncle, John Meller, whose refurnishing of the house he had helped to supervise. He himself did little to the building.

BRITISH, 1835
Simon Yorke III (1811–94)
Painted the year after he inherited Erddig from his father, Simon II. He rarely left the estate, which he changed little.

FRANCIS COTES, RA (1726–70)
Elizabeth Cust, Mrs Yorke (1750–79)
Younger daughter of Sir John Cust, Speaker of the House of Commons, of Belton, Lincolnshire (also NT), she married Philip Yorke I as his first wife in 1770, the probable date of this picture. The crook garlanded with flowers certainly suggests that it is a marriage portrait.

Attributed to WILLIAM HOARE of Bath (1707/8–92)
Anne Jemima Yorke (1754–70)
Pastel
The musical daughter of Simon Yorke I and sister-in-law of the above. The white dress, garlanded urn and probable date of 1770 all suggest the portrait is posthumous.

BRITISH SCHOOL (*c*.1840/50)
General the Hon. Sir Edward Cust (1794–1878)
The father of Victoria Cust, who married Simon Yorke III in 1846. General, courtier, military historian and Christian writer.

Rev. JAMES WILLS (active 1740–77)
Philip Yorke, 1st Earl of Hardwicke (1690–1764)
His uncle Simon established the Yorke line at Erddig, through his marriage with Anne, the sister of John Meller. Painted in his robes as Lord Chancellor (1737–56), he bought Wimpole Hall, Cambridgeshire (also NT) in 1740.

Studio of FRANS SNYDERS (1597–1657)
Still-life with a Servant and a Dog
The original is in the Statens Museum for Kunst, Copenhagen. From the collection of Simon Yorke I's brother-in-law, James Hutton.

? CHARLES JERVAS (*c.*1675–1739) and THOMAS GAINSBOROUGH, RA (1727–88)
John Meller (1665–1733)
A prosperous lawyer, he bought Erddig in 1716, adding the two wings between 1721 and 1724, and introducing much of the superb furniture still in the house, which he bequeathed to his nephew, Simon Yorke I. Painted *c.*1715 and drastically reworked in 1780 by Gainsborough, who retained only the face and background.

JACQUELINE GELDART
Simon Yorke IV (1903–66)
Signed and dated 1977
Penultimate owner of Erddig and sullen enemy of the National Coal Board, whose workings were undermining the house. Painted posthumously from a photograph taken in 1936.

JACQUELINE GELDART
Philip Yorke III (1905–78)
Signed and dated 1977
Tour operator, actor-manager and last squire of Erddig. He did much to preserve the decaying house, finally giving it to the National Trust in 1973.

LOUIS WILLIAM DESANGES (b.1822)
Philip Yorke II (1849–1922)
He spent much of his early life travelling and settled at Erddig only after the death in 1899 of his first wife, from whom he was separated. His care for the staff and for the contents of Erddig did much to preserve its special character.

GILBERT BALDRY
Louisa Scott, Mrs Yorke (1863–1951)
Dated (on frame) 1906
Daughter of the Rev. T. Scott, vicar of Chilton Foliat, Wiltshire, and second wife of Philip Yorke II, whom she married in 1902. They shared an enthusiasm for cycling.

After GEORGE ROMNEY (1734–1802)
Sir Brownlow Cust, Baron Brownlow (1744–1807)
A friend at Cambridge of Philip Yorke I, who married his sister Elizabeth (above) in 1770. He inherited Belton the same year and was raised to the peerage in 1776 in memory of his famous father, Speaker Cust. The original is at Belton.

THOMAS GAINSBOROUGH, RA (1727–88)
Philip Yorke I, MP (1743–1804)
Son of Simon Yorke I. High Sheriff of Denbighshire in 1786 and MP for Helston and Grantham, he was more interested in books than politics, writing *The Royal Tribes of Wales* (1799). He began the famous series of servant portraits in the 1790s. Probably painted in the late 1770s.

GILBERT BALDRY
Simon Yorke III (1811–94)
The owner of Victorian Erddig in old age. Said to have been painted from a photograph.

BRITISH, *c.*1815
Margaret Yorke (1778–1848) and her eldest son?, Simon III (1811–94)
Margaret Holland married Simon Yorke II in 1807. Although the label identifies the child as her eldest daughter, Anne (b.1810), it is more likely to be her first-born son. Painted by a provincial artist, perhaps John Walters, the author of the Servants' Hall portraits.

STATUETTES

ON CHIMNEYPIECE:

SEBASTIAN SLODTZ (1655–1726)
Mars and *Venus*
Bronze

Attributed to MICHAEL ANGUIER
Pluto
Bronze

CURTAINS

The ornate gilt curtain rods were supplied by Gillow of Lancaster in the 1820s, although the curtains themselves date from the 1970s. The latter were designed by John Fowler, following some original Gillow drawings.

FURNITURE

The set of 22 mahogany dining-chairs was given to Simon Yorke II and his wife Margaret as a present by her brother, John Holland, in 1827. They were made by Gillow, and the chairs still retain their original red morocco leather upholstery.

The oak longcase clock was made by John Smith of Wrexham *c.*1826.

AT EACH END OF THE ROOM:

Two Regency serving-tables. On the far table sits a pair of mahogany-veneered knife boxes with serpentine fronts and silver mounts of about 1770; the cutlery itself bears the Yorke crest.

ON WINDOW WALL:

A Victorian overmantel glass is hung above a late Georgian mahogany sideboard. According to Louisa Matilda Yorke, the glass was bought locally in 1908 for £5.

TEXTILES

The Turkey carpet was, according to Louisa Yorke, acquired in 1902 for £10.

The Indian embroidered panel of wool and metal thread was bought for 18s in Wrexham.

CISTERN

IN FAR LEFT CORNER:

The Georgian marble wine cistern with gadrooned decoration may be the one supplied by the London mason and stone-carver John Deval in 1772. It was filled with 20 gallons or so of punch on the occasion of Simon Yorke II's coming-of-age party in 1792.

METALWORK

The two-handled silver cup and cover of 1787 was made by Daniel Smith and Robert Sharp and presented to Simon Yorke III, who was Captain of the Denbighshire Rifle Volunteers between 1862 and 1879.

The nickel-plated sweet-pea bowl was awarded in 1908 to Philip Yorke II and Mr Aitkin, head gardener.

WEIGHTS AND MEASURES

BY NEAR COLUMNS:

A pair of oak barrels, made by a Wrexham cooper in 1910. Each supports a bronze bushel measure, one inscribed with the Meller crest and stating that it was used to collect the toll within the town of Wrexham in 1716. The other, dated 1663, was found by Louisa Yorke in the estate paint shop in 1903, where it had lain for many years.

ON AND UNDER SIDEBOARD:

The other weights and measures were made by John Smart for John Meller in 1716. They were used for measuring corn at the Kingsmill in Wrexham, an important part of the Erddig estate.

TURTLE

The stuffed and lacquered Hawksbill Turtle (Eret-mochelys imbricata) was probably washed up on the North Wales coast. The shell of the Hawksbill was commonly used for making tortoiseshell objects.

THE SALOON

The saloon of Edisbury and Meller's house was about two-thirds the size of the present one, occupying the area furthest from the Dining Room. The smaller area was occupied by the Withdrawing Room, the first element in a typical Baroque apartment, with the Best Bedchamber (now the Dining Room) beyond.

In 1771 Philip Yorke I created a larger saloon by removing the partition between the two rooms, but he took care to retain the late seventeenth-century oak panelling with bolection mouldings. (The old division can still be discerned in the

The Saloon

A watercolour of the Saloon in 1849

panelling opposite the garden door.) The result was a symmetrical five-bayed room with matching chimneypieces.

CEILING

The decorative ceiling is made up of pressed steel panels. It dates from the early twentieth century, when it was introduced as a fire precaution.

PICTURES

BRITISH, mid-eighteenth-century
Jane Seymour (1509–37)
Copper
Wife of Henry VIII and mother of Edward VI.

BRITISH, mid-eighteenth-century
Henry VIII (1491–1547)
Copper
Pendant of the above.

UNKNOWN ARTIST
Expulsion of Adam and Eve

DUTCH, late seventeenth-century
A Still-life with Flowers

After CASPAR NETSCHER (1639–84)
Princesses Albertina Agnes (1634–96) *and Henrietta Catherina* (1637–1708) *of Orange-Nassau*
Daughters of Frederick Henry, Prince of Orange (hence the orange), and Amalia van Solms.

UNKNOWN ARTIST
Dead Game

Manner of JAN WYCK (c.1640–1702)
William III (1650–1702) *giving orders in the field*
From James Hutton's collection.

Manner of PANDOLFO RESCHI (c.1643/4–99)
Battle Scene with Horsemen and Foot Soldiers
From Hutton's collection.

Manner of PAULUS POTTER (1625–54)
Four Cows by the water's edge with a Boy in a Boat
Bears Potter's signature and date 166[?]
Probably a nineteenth-century pastiche.

FURNITURE

The room houses some of the finest pieces of furniture purchased by John Meller in the 1720s from leading London cabinetmakers. The arrangement has not changed substantially since the 1770s, although successive generations of Yorkes made minor alterations and added contemporary pieces. The current arrangement is based on the appearance of the Saloon in the late nineteenth century.

The set of eight carved and silvered chairs and matching settee in 1726 formed part of the furnishings of the Withdrawing Room to the Best Bedchamber (now part of the Saloon). Each is upholstered in crimson Spitalfields cut velvet, which is almost identical to that on a contemporary set of seat furniture at Powis Castle, Powys. By the nineteenth century the silvered surfaces had been overpainted with gold to match the gilded girandoles in the Saloon. The original silvering on the settee was restored by Edward Davies in 1910 and that on the chairs was carefully uncovered during the restoration of the 1970s.

IN CENTRE OF WEST WALL (FACING WINDOWS):

A Boulle bureau or dressing-table of about 1695, veneered with brass and tortoiseshell. It was purchased by Meller and originally stood between the windows in the Best Bedchamber. Philip Yorke I introduced it into the Saloon in the 1770s.

FLANKING BUREAU:

A pair of gilded sconces or girandoles, which are among the largest and finest of their kind. These are listed in an inventory of 1726 and were originally hung on the window wall of the original, smaller Saloon. They were probably the work of John Pardoe (active 1710–48). A bill received from Pardoe in September 1720 describes 'a paire of large looking glass sconces' for £12 10s. They are, however, close in form to a silvered sconce in the Tapestry Room supplied by John Belchier, cabinetmaker 'at ye Sun in St. Paul's Churchyard'.

ON WINDOW WALL:

Two tall giltwood pier-glasses, also supplied by Belchier and listed in bills of the 1720s. The larger of these, with the more richly carved cresting and two profile heads, was bought by Meller in 1726 for £50 and is probably the 'very large glass' referred to in the 1726 inventory, when it hung in the Best Bedchamber above the Boulle bureau. Its slightly smaller companion, surmounted by a plumed human mask, was acquired by Meller three years before for £36 and is likely to be the glass described in the Second Best Bedchamber in 1726. It probably hung above the gilt gesso side-table, with unusual scrolled, shell-like feet, which now stands in the Tapestry Room.

BELOW:

The nineteenth-century pier-tables have eighteenth-century marble tops and may be part of the 'two marble tables with walnut tree fraims' referred to in the 1726 inventory.

The pelmets of crimson silk damask survive from the mid-nineteenth century, although the curtains themselves are modern copies. In the 1720s, the two windows of the original Withdrawing Room were hung with crimson velvet curtains to match the silvered furniture. The effect must have been striking.

The surviving seat furniture from Meller's Saloon is now to be found in the Gallery.

Later eighteenth-century furniture, introduced by Philip Yorke I, includes:

Four mahogany armchairs in the French taste, probably made by John Cobb (d.1778), the celebrated cabinetmaker and upholsterer of St Martin's Lane, London.

An Irish Chippendale side-table, the apron boldly carved with a scrolling leaf pattern and with a scalloped shell centre.

A Chelsea plaice tureen, c.1756 (Saloon)

Nineteenth-century pieces include:

ON SOUTH WALL:

A large vitrine, bought to complement the Boulle bureau, with two smaller ones on the west wall containing ceramics (see below) and an early nineteenth-century French bracket clock with cast and chased ormolu mounts by Nicolas de Lannay.

Part of a large set of Maplewood Rout chairs.

TEXTILES

The Axminster carpet with a stylised diamond trellis pattern of blue and green flowers was bought by Simon Yorke III in about 1859. By 1906 it had been badly attacked by moth but was repaired by Lousia Yorke with wool bought in Wrexham.

GLASS AND CERAMICS

The George III cut-glass chandelier has been in this room since 1846, having been given to Simon Yorke III and Victoria Cust as a wedding present by Lady Brownlow. It was badly broken in 1903 by the butler who, when cleaning it, spun it round so often that it became unthreaded and crashed to the floor. It was repaired with Bohemian glass by Sherratts of Chester in 1904 at a cost of £38.

ON CHIMNEYPIECE:

Garniture of three Delft fluted polychrome vases in the Chinese manner, eighteenth-century.

ON BRACKETS:

A pair of Worcester vases and covers c.1770.

IN LEFT-HAND BOULLE VITRINE:

Four Urbino maiolica plates, one of which (dated 1543) depicts Camilla, a warrior maiden who features in Virgil's *Aeneid*. The others are later sixteenth-century.

Chocolate cups, with Chelsea red anchor marks, *c.*1755–8.

A glass beaker with engraved coats of arms, commemorating the marriage of Simon Yorke I and Dorothy Hutton in 1739.

IN RIGHT-HAND BOULLE VITRINE:

A late seventeenth-century ceremonial goblet, belonging to a small and interesting group of such pieces.

A pair of Chelsea plaice tureens, covers and stands, which matches the description in the 1756 Chelsea sale catalogue of 'a beautiful pair of place sauceboats with spoons and plates'. They may be the '2 stands and two carp [sic] Sauce Boats 6 pieces in all' listed in the 1789 inventory.

Eight Chinese plates painted with *The Judgement of Paris.* They are mentioned in the 1770 inventory of the Yorkes' London house and possibly in the 1789 Erddig inventory. Louisa Yorke considered them improper and hid them at the back of the cabinet.

A Chelsea blue ground écuelle and cover, painted in the style of John Donaldson with musical couples, *c.*1765.

Asparagus servers with Chelsea red anchor marks, *c.*1755–8.

ON BOULLE VITRINE ON SOUTH WALL:

A pair of early nineteenth-century English vases copying Meissen, modelled with yellow birds on blossoming branches, possibly Derby.

IN BOULLE VITRINE:

A small Worcester mug with a black transfer print of Frederick the Great, one of the '3 Kings of Prussia cupps' in the 1789 inventory.

ON BOULLE BUREAU:

A pair of Meissen two-handled baluster vases, late nineteenth-century.

PICTURE

BETWEEN SALOON AND TAPESTRY ROOM:

B–B–
The Saloon at Erddig, 1849
Inscribed: *B.B./Aug^t/[4?]9*
Watercolour
Shows the room much as today, but with more porcelain, and before the introduction of the Boulle china cabinets.

THE TAPESTRY ROOM

This room was originally the 'Second Best Bed Chamber' of Meller's 1720s house. Like the other ground-floor rooms it was altered by Philip Yorke I in the 1770s, when he introduced the Soho tapestries (see below), which had previously hung in the 'Best Bed Chamber', a room almost identical in size to this.

The oak panelling dates from the early eighteenth century. The unusual pressed steel ceiling, like that in the Saloon, is one of six introduced in the early twentieth century as a form of fire prevention.

TAPESTRIES

The set of Soho tapestries was commissioned by Meller in about 1720 for the Best Bedchamber. Simon Yorke I supervised their delivery to Erddig (see p.12). The central scenes, set within decorative borders of fruit and exotic birds, have traditionally been identified with the biblical story of Solomon and Sheba, but seem to be more generalised and non-narrative in character. The figures, shown eating and playing music in elaborate outdoor settings, may have been inspired by African, Chinese or other exotic sources. Three from the original set of four are hung here; one is in store.

FURNITURE

The layout reflects the character of the room during its Edwardian heyday, when it was primarily used as a room of display for the Soho tapestries and the Delft vase.

The Tapestry Room

BETWEEN WINDOWS:

The large silvered pier-glass, for which John Belchier was paid £21 in 1723, was intended to complement the silvered suite of seat furniture in Meller's Withdrawing Room. It too was overpainted in gold in the nineteenth century and restored by the National Trust.

BELOW:

The carved and silvered gesso pier-table is the 'silver table with glass top and Coats of Arms, cut and gilt in itt' which was supplied to Meller in 1726. The mirrored top with Meller's heraldic device painted in *verre églomisé* (painted glass) was badly damaged in 1853 when Philip Yorke II, then aged four, smashed it with a toy hammer he had been given as a birthday present.

A carved and gilt gesso side-table. Probably the 'gold table and leather cover' mentioned as being in this room in 1726.

BESIDE THE FIREPLACE:

A nineteenth-century antiquarian fire-screen with a late seventeenth-century embroidered panel depicting Susannah and the Elders.

CERAMICS

The large Delft vase is of particular interest. It bears the royal arms of William and Mary and is probably one of those made by Adriaen Kocks *c.*1690–1700 for Hampton Court, resembling designs for such vases by Daniel Marot. By family tradition, it was a present from Queen Anne to Mrs Wanley, a relation of the Hutton family. It was probably brought to Erddig in 1787 and was listed here in 1805.

THE CHINESE ROOM

This formed the dressing-room of the 'Second Best Bed Chamber' until the late eighteenth century, when Philip Yorke I transformed it into a 'porcelain cabinet' and hung the walls with Chinese wallpaper. The hand-painted vignettes illustrate various ways of earning a living: three on the window wall are English copies. The surrounding block-printed borders of flowers and butterflies are European.

Through the door in the small area beyond, which was known as the Flower Room, the Yorkes gained access to the family pew in the Chapel. In the late nineteenth century the room was used by

The Chinese Room

Victoria Yorke as a boudoir and many of the furnishings were introduced by her. A photograph of her hangs above the door from the Tapestry Room.

PICTURES

The walls are hung with a series of watercolours and small oil paintings, including *High Life* and *Low Life*, both painted in 1877 by Philip Yorke II, and a pair of portraits of the Rev. Thomas James Scott and Mrs Sophia Ann Scott, his parents-in-law.

KATHERINE READ (1723–78)

Simon Yorke II (1771–1834) *and his sister Etheldred* (1772–96)
Pastel; oval
The two eldest children of Philip Yorke I, by his first wife, Elizabeth Cust. Read was a fashionable Scottish portraitist, mainly in pastel, who worked in London from 1754. This must have been painted shortly before she left for India in 1775.

FURNITURE

FLANKING FIREPLACE:

The walnut bookcases were made by one of the Erddig carpenters for Victoria Yorke out of earlier pieces.

ABOVE FIREPLACE:

The 'landskip' glass is probably one of four supplied for the house in 1723–4 by Belchier and is flanked by the original glass candle arms.

Pairs of early nineteenth-century green and gilt decorated brackets with trefoil-shaped shells, the lower supported by a pineapple motif.

IN CORNER:

A late nineteenth-century box Ottoman with upholstery made by Victoria Yorke.

The early eighteenth-century black japanned corner cupboard was given to Victoria Yorke by her children as a birthday present.

The eighteenth-century French ormolu and crystal chandelier is one of a pair (the other is in the Drawing Room). According to Louisa Yorke, they were purchased at a sale in Bournemouth for £5 5s.

The small eighteenth-century Dutch walnut marquetry cabinet is probably an apprentice's piece and was purchased about 1908 for £5.

CERAMICS

ON BOOKCASES BESIDE FIREPLACE:

Two Japanese Buddhist Rakan (disciples), second half of seventeenth century. Listed in 1789 as 'China beggar men with stands'.

IN DUTCH MARQUETRY CABINET:

A collection of blue-and-white porcelain, some of which may be that described in the 1726 inventory.

A Chelsea broth bowl and cover, painted with exotic birds possibly by J. H. O'Neale, and perhaps the 'Syllabub cup' listed in the 1789 inventory.

THE LIBRARY

The Library was not created until 1775, when Philip Yorke I altered and enlarged what had been the Little Parlour of Edisbury's 1680s house. In that year he brought down the collection of books from Meller's Study, a room situated above the Chinese Room.

BOOKS

According to Louisa Yorke, the 1,500 or so volumes were arranged and catalogued by Victoria Yorke and her father, Sir Edward Cust, between 1848 and 1850, and then again in 1902 by herself and her friends, the Misses Robinson, after many spring cleanings had upset the order. The collection contains good standard volumes of the kind frequently found in a country gentleman's library with few outstanding or rare items, although there are rather more legal books than usual – a reflection of Meller's profession. Curiously, the stacks are marked, and the volumes arranged, from right to left – the reverse of the normal practice.

PICTURES

HUNG AROUND WALLS AND SHELVES:

A selection of engravings of the Yorkes and their kinsmen and documents, including the design of about 1778 for the stained-glass windows of nearby Marchwiel church, for which James Wyatt designed a tower erected by Philip Yorke I in 1788.

The Library

JOSEPH ALLEN (1769–1839)

Twelve wash drawings after portraits at Erddig, Chirk Castle, also in Clwyd, and elsewhere, commissioned by Philip Yorke I while preparing his *The Royal Tribes of Wales* (1799):

Humphrey Stafford or Bagot, 1st Duke of Buckingham, KG (1402–60)

Catherine of Berain (1535–91)

Sir Thomas Egerton, Viscount Brackley (1540–1617)

Sir John Vaughan (1603–74)

Sir Orlando Bridgeman (1606?-74)

Sir Thomas Myddelton, KG (1586–1666)

George, 1st Baron Jeffreys of Wem (1648–89)

Sir Thomas Hanmer, 4th Bt (1677–1746)

Sir John Trevor of Brynkinalt (1637–1717)

William Williams, 1st Bt (1634–1700)

Humphrey Lloyd (1527–68)

Sir John Wynn, 5th Bt, of Wynnstay (1627/8–1718/19)

BETTY RATCLIFFE (c.1735-c.1810)
Unknown man, called William Shakespeare
Pencil

FURNITURE

The mahogany library table in the manner of Thomas Chippendale was used by Philip Yorke I from 1770. On it is a Regency black marble inkstand made by B. Vulliamy with an assortment of paperweights and knives.

AROUND ROOM:

The set of walnut side-chairs is probably that described in the 1726 inventory as being in John Meller's 'Breakfast Room'. They are of two different designs, having vase-shaped splats with inset panels of 'seaweed marquetry'.

Other eighteenth-century pieces include:

The walnut veneered card- or tea-table of c.1720.

The pier-glasses with bevelled glass borders were probably supplied by John Belchier. The frames are japanned and gilded with rosettes and trellis-work.

The pair of terrestrial and celestial globes was made c.1750 by W. and T. M. Bardin of Fleet Street.

ON NORTH WALL:

The mid-nineteenth-century set of bookshelves was made from earlier pieces of woodwork. It may have come from Plas Newydd, Llangollen, the home of Simon III's brother, General John Yorke (see p.23).

The oak cigar cabinet was made by the estate joiner William Gittins and given by Louisa Yorke and her children to Philip Yorke II at Christmas 1908. Inside, a label explains that the legs and framing were made from pieces of the old staircase from Hafod y Bwlch, the side panels from a piece of furniture from the Estate Office, the small brackets out of an old drawer from the attic and the lid from an old panel from the hall of nearby Plas Grono.

The Regency bronze hanging lamp with four burners originally had glass globes and was fuelled by Colza oil, a vegetable oil derived from oil seed rape. In 1902 it was converted for paraffin.

THE ENTRANCE HALL
(MUSIC ROOM)

This room served as the principal Entrance Hall until the late nineteenth century, when the Yorkes began to use the lower ground-floor Tribes Room as a more convenient and less draughty entrance. It then became a music room, although always called simply 'the Hall'.

In the 1770s Philip Yorke I had remodelled the room to create a strictly symmetrical space, blocking up a door on the east wall (behind the pier-glass) which had led directly into the Saloon, introducing

Matthew Hutton (d.1728); by John Verelst, 1715 (Entrance Hall). His Newnham estate passed to the Yorkes in 1770

a false door (behind the piano), and making a door in the south wall into what was to become the Drawing Room. The Hall was stripped of its original panelling, and light Neo-classical decoration was introduced. The alterations have been attributed to James Wyatt: he was certainly consulted by Philip Yorke I in the 1770s and craftsmen with whom he regularly collaborated received payments for interior work at Erddig. The plaster frieze with anthemion motif was executed in August–September 1773 by Joseph Rose & Company, the most celebrated plasterers of their day. The chimneypiece was supplied by the workshop of John Devall the Younger (1728–94), a mason closely associated with Wyatt.

PICTURES

FACING WINDOWS:

Sir GODFREY KNELLER, Bt (1646/9–1723)
George, 1st Baron Jeffreys of Wem (1648–89)
The infamous judge. Following the defeat of the

Monmouth Rebellion in 1685, he sentenced around 150 of the rebels to death in the 'bloody assizes'. He is shown in his robes as Baron Jeffreys, which he was created in 1685 by James II. He was Lord Chancellor from September 1685 until the King's overthrow in 1688, and died in the Tower of London the following year.

? Sir GODFREY KNELLER, Bt (1646/9–1723) and Studio
Sir Thomas Jeffreys
An elder brother of Judge Jeffreys, he became a Catholic and served as a consul in Spain. Painted while he was in England, 1686–7 (like the portrait of his brother). He wears the robes of the Order of Alcantara.

BRITISH, early eighteenth-century
Margaret Dodwell, Mrs Southcomb
Oval
Daughter of Dr Henry and Ann Dodwell, who were possibly forebears of Margaret Holland, the wife of Simon Yorke II.

JOHN VERELST (active 1698–1734)
Matthew Hutton of Newnham, Hertfordshire (d.1728)
Signed and dated 1715
His daughter and heir Dorothy married Simon Yorke I in 1739. The wealth that the Yorkes inherited in 1770 on the death of Hutton's son James transformed the family's fortunes.

OVER FIREPLACE:

After Sir PETER LELY (1618–80)
Charles II (1630–85)
Contemporary copy of the portrait at Euston Hall, Suffolk, showing the King in his Garter robes.

JOHN VERELST (active 1698–1734)
Mrs Matthew Hutton
Signed and dated 1715
Pendant to the picture on the other side of the fireplace.

Follower of Sir GODFREY KNELLER, Bt
(1646/9–1723)
Dorothy Taylor, Mrs William Kinaston

Attributed to THOMAS MURRAY (1663–1754)
William Kinaston the Younger of Ruyton Hall, Shropshire
Pendant to the above.

ENOCH SEEMAN (c.1694–1744/5)
Elizabeth Cartwright, Viscountess Tyrconnel (d.1780)
Daughter of William Cartwright of Marnham,

The Entrance Hall

Nottinghamshire, she married in 1732, as his second wife, Sir John Brownlow, Viscount Tyrconnel. Companion to Kneller's portrait of Tyrconnel, below.

RIGHT OF ORGAN:

Sir GODFREY KNELLER, Bt (1646/9–1723)
Sir John Brownlow, Viscount Tyrconnel (1690–1754)
Signed and dated 1720
Picture-collector, patron of the arts and frustrated politician. He was the nephew of 'Young Sir John' Brownlow, the builder of Belton, which he inherited in 1702. His grand-niece Elizabeth Cust married Philip Yorke I. Painted the year after he was created Viscount Tyrconnel.

BRITISH, early eighteenth-century
An Unknown Lady (? Mrs Ann Dodwell)
Oval
Possibly the mother of Margaret Southcomb (above) in half-mourning. It is apparently by the same hand and presumably painted as a companion to it.

FURNITURE

In the early eighteenth century the room had been furnished with ten black leather chairs, marble-topped tables against each of the window piers, backgammon and ombre tables, and a gilded screen to provide some protection from draughts.

ON WEST (WINDOW) WALL:

The pier-glasses, c.1720, with walnut-veneered frames, were probably supplied by John Belchier. The shape of the upper plate and the inverted widow's peak at the apex are similar to that found on one of the gilded pier-glasses in the Saloon.

ON OPPOSITE (EAST) WALL:

An ebonised and giltwood pier-glass and table in a Rococo revival style, bought at a sale in Wrexham in 1905.

The set of six Hepplewhite period chairs with interlaced splats was purchased in 1880 in Chester by Victoria Yorke.

The rectangular oak refectory table, the upper part of which is sixteenth-century, was discovered in the pigsty in 1900 and repaired by John Jones, the Erddig joiner, in 1919. He made a top from a piece of oak panelling removed from the attic after a fire and repaired the frieze. He also pieced in new sections to the legs to designs by Philip Yorke II.

The early Victorian ormolu chandelier was probably a wedding present to Simon and Victoria Yorke in 1846 from Lady Brownlow. It was later fitted with Colza oil lamps and in 1903 converted for paraffin.

The ormolu bracket clock in French-Egyptian style signed 'Rieusset H Gen du Roy' was inherited by Philip Yorke III from the Yorke Lodge family.

The Victorian mahogany ebonised display cabinet contains a number of silver trophies and christening pieces presented by Simon IV and Philip III Yorke.

MUSICAL INSTRUMENTS

The chamber organ was purchased in 1865 by Philip Yorke II, then aged 15, for £227 2s 4d, using a legacy of £100 from his godfather; the balance was found by his father. It was made by Bevington & Sons, London, a firm specialising in moderately sized and smaller organs. The Victorian Gothic case, with croqueted finials, pierced frieze and polychromed decoration to the pipes and the end panels, resembles many contemporary ecclesiastical instruments. Also by Bevingtons is the 'dumb' organist, a mechanical organ player.

The Klems baby grand piano was bought in Stuttgart for £45 by Philip Yorke II in the 1870s, while he was a student in Germany.

The harp lute, c.1810, with black lacquered body and applied gilt transfer decoration, was made by Edward Light of London.

The brass euphonium was made by J. Higham Ltd in the late nineteenth century.

ON TABLE IN CENTRE OF ROOM:

A number of mechanical musical players, including an automaton of an old man playing an upright piano made in France c.1900, and a cylindrical musical box in a rosewood case which played twelve tunes. The 'Polygon' musical box with metal discs and the 'Ariston' pneumatic musical disc player with cardboard discs were both made at the turn of the century. The Edison Standard Phonograph with sound horn from New Jersey played cylindrical vinyl records in cardboard tubes.

CERAMICS

ON GILTWOOD PIER-TABLE:

A set of three Chinese famille verte hexagonal vases and covers, K'ang Hsi period, c.1700.

A pair of large Japanese Imari vases and covers, c.1700–20, with stands made during Wyatt's redecoration of the room in the 1770s.

Two Chinese brown biscuit hawks, mid-eighteenth-century.

THE DRAWING ROOM

Formerly Meller's Eating Parlour, this room, like the Entrance Hall, was remodelled in a Neo-classical style by Philip Yorke I in 1773, with plasterwork by Joseph Rose's team and a carved marble fireplace attributed to John Devall. The present colour scheme, and the arrangement of the room as a picture cabinet, is broadly based on a description in Louisa Yorke's *Facts and Fancies* (1923). The last Philip Yorke used it as a bed-sitting room (as can be seen in the photograph on the piano).

Classical Landscape with Mercury, Herse and Aglaurus; attributed to Jan Glauber (Drawing Room)

PICTURES

WEST (WINDOW) WALL, RIGHT PIER, TOP TO BOTTOM:

FLORENTINE, ? sixteenth-century
Christ succoured by Angels in the Wilderness, after the Temptation
Copper

Manner of JAN BRUEGHEL I (1568–1625)
River Scene with Boats
Copper

? GASPARD DUGHET (1615–75)
Landscape with Travellers and a Distant River Valley
Framed as a pendant to the picture only in the manner of Dughet, but possibly an authentic late work by this artist.

LEFT PIER, TOP TO BOTTOM:

BRITISH, mid-eighteenth-century
Clifton Rocks
A view of the River Avon west of Bristol.

ITALIAN, *c.*1700
Landscape with Figures

GASPARD DUGHET (1615–75), manner of
L'ORIZZONTE (1662–1749)
Two Men Conversing by a Lake Beneath a Castle

SOUTH (FAR) WALL, TOP ROW:

FLEMISH-ITALIAN, *c.*1700
Landscape with Diana at the Chase
From James Hutton's collection.

? FLEMISH, early seventeenth-century
Kitchen Scene and Still-life

JAN FRANS VAN BLOEMEN, called
L'ORIZZONTE (1662–1749)
A Woman Conversing with Two Men on a Path

MIDDLE ROW:

After PHILIPPE MERCIER (1689–1760)
Wilks as Captain Plume in 'The Recruiting Officer'
Metal
Act III, scene I of George Farquhar's play (1706). Plume attempts to seduce Rose, and to enlist her brother, Bullock, into the army. Sergeant Kite sits with a glass of wine.

*The last Philip Yorke in the Drawing Room a few
months before he gave Erddig to the National Trust*

Attributed to JOSEPH VAN AKEN (*c.*1699–1749)
A Group of Gentlemen Drinking
The man in the turban may be a self-portrait of the
artist.
From James Hutton's collection.

BOTTOM ROW:

FLEMISH, seventeenth-century
An Extensive Landscape
Canvas laid on panel

BRITISH, eighteenth-century
An Unknown Lady called 'Mary Tudor'
An eighteenth-century pastiche of a sixteenth-cen-
tury portrait.

NETHERLANDISH, *c.*1700
Buildings by a River
Panel

NETHERLANDISH, *c.*1700
Buildings by a River
Panel

DUTCH, seventeenth-century
? *Chief Justice Sir John Glynne* (1603–66)
Panel; oval
The identification is traditional.

FLEMISH-ITALIAN, *c.*1700
Classical Landscape with Ruins and Women
Canvas laid on panel

EAST (FACING WINDOW) WALL, TOP ROW:

Attributed to JAN GLAUBER (1646–*c.*1726)
Classical Landscape with Mercury, Herse and Aglaurus
The sisters Herse and Aglaurus return from the
festival of Minerva and are seen by the god
Mercury, who falls in love with Herse.

? JEAN-BAPTISTE MONNOYER (1636–99)
Still-life with Flowers
From James Hutton's collection.

The Hon. ELIZABETH CUST (1776–1858) after
ELIZABETH SIRANI (1638–65)
Girl with a Basket of Doves
Painted by the niece of the Elizabeth Cust who
married Philip Yorke I. She catalogued the picture
collection at Belton and was a talented copyist.

? JOSEPH VAN DER VOORT (active 1714–54/5)
Landscape with Huntsmen
Inscribed: ? *P. Vandervoorde I¹ et f¹ A° 171[6?]*

After AMBROSIUS BENSON (active *c*.1515–d.1550)
The Magdalen
The original is in the Royal Collection.

BOTTOM ROW:

Manner of NICOLAES BERCHEM (1620–83)
Farmyard with Cattle and Figures

DUTCH, seventeenth-century
Still-life with Food and Drink
Panel

After ? MARCELLO VENUSTI (1512/15–79)
Christ and the Woman of Samaria
Christ asks the Samaritan woman for a drink from
the well, much to her astonishment because of the
traditional hatred between their two races: 'Whoever drinks the water I shall give him will never
suffer thirst any more.' Derived ultimately from a
lost painting by Michelangelo.

NORTH (FIREPLACE) WALL, TOP ROW:

? DUTCH, seventeenth- or eighteenth-century
Still-life with Peaches
From James Hutton's collection.

Manner of PIETER SNAYERS (1592–1667)
A Cavalry Battle

BRITISH, eighteenth-century
Still-life with Parrot and Fruit
From James Hutton's collection.

BOTTOM ROW:

DUTCH, seventeenth- or eighteenth-century
Still-life with Lemons

FURNITURE

ABOVE FIREPLACE:

The early eighteenth-century chimney glass may have
been supplied to Meller by John Belchier.

RIGHT OF FIREPLACE:

The pole-screen with the shield-shaped needlework
panel was embroiderd by Victoria Yorke.

ON EAST WALL (OPPOSITE):

*An early eighteenth-century chinoiserie black lacquered
cabinet* with elaborate brass mounts.

The boudoir grand pianoforte was made by Collard &
Collard.

ON FAR (SOUTH) WALL:

The mid-Georgian mahogany glazed cabinet was
bought in 1904.

The eighteenth-century French chandelier is paired with
one in the Chinese Room bought in Bournemouth
for £5 5s, as was the Persian carpet of about
1900.

The set of 1770s mahogany settee and chairs in the
French style was probably supplied to Philip Yorke
I by the cabinetmaker John Cobb. They have been
reupholstered in black horse hair by the National
Trust.

THE SOUTH INNER HALL
AND STAIRS

Although essentially the back stairs of the house, this
area was used as a main thoroughfare.

FURNITURE

The oak court cupboard with carved front is Jacobean
and probably Welsh in origin.

The set of eight tubular bells suspended from a
mahogany frame dates from 1900.

The pair of varnished oak hall-chairs is carved with the
Scott crest.

CERAMICS

ON SHELVES:

*Mostly Chinese famille rose and blue-and-white por-
celain* of the Quianlong period (1736–95).

A pair of square Derby bowls in the Japanese Arita
style, *c*.1760.

PICTURES

JOSEPH ALLEN (1769–1839) after JONATHAN
RICHARDSON (1664/5–1745)
Sir Robert Walpole, 1st Earl of Orford (1676–1745)
The first Prime Minister (1715–17, 1721–42), por-
trayed in green hunting dress as Deputy Ranger of
Richmond Park.

Sir FRANCIS GRANT, PRA (1803–78)
Mathilda, Mrs Holland (d.1905)
Wife of the below. According to Grant's sitter
book, painted in 1858. She is shown in mourning.

Sir FRANCIS GRANT, PRA (1803–78)
The Rev. William Holland (d.1878)
Rector of Cold Norton, Essex. Painted in 1851.

THE RED BEDROOM

The lobby into the Red Bedroom is hung with a late
nineteenth-century machine-printed wallpaper of
peacocks. The door to the right leads to the former
nurseries. During the remodelling of the Dining
Room by Thomas Hopper in the 1820s, the Red
Bedroom was repanelled (perhaps reusing some of
the discarded wainscot). Later in the century it
became a bedroom, with an adjoining dressing-
room, for Victoria Yorke.

PICTURES

The two cut-out paper silhouettes on red foil background were made by Betty Ratcliffe, lady's maid
and companion to Dorothy Yorke, mother of
Philip Yorke I (see p.68). One depicts the arms of
the Yorke and Hutton families, the other Yorke and
Cust; the latter was probably made to celebrate
Philip's marriage to Elizabeth Cust in 1770.

The Raphael cartoons. The seven engravings after the
cartoons in the Royal Collection are mentioned in
the inventory of 1726.

BRITISH, eighteenth-century
The Bird's Nester
Labelled as of Matthew Hutton, father of James
Hutton, from whose collection it came. However, it
is not a portrait, but copied from a seventeenth-
century original, which is perhaps by Isaac Fuller.

*The arms of Yorke and Hutton; cut-paper silhouette by
Betty Ratcliffe (Red Bedroom)*

After Sir GODFREY KNELLER, Bt (1646/9–1723)
Prince William Henry, Duke of Gloucester, KG
(1689–1700)
The eldest son of Queen Anne and the only one of
her many children to survive infancy.

FURNITURE

The Chippendale period mahogany four-poster bed of
about 1760 is traditionally said to have been
designed for Philip Yorke I's sister, Anne Jemima,
who died of consumption in 1770, aged sixteen. It
incorporates a mechanism for raising the head of the
bed or lifting one side of it. The bed-hangings were
renewed in the mid-nineteenth century and largely
survive.

The late Georgian oak hanging cupboard, marked 'G.R.
1719', was accepted by the Yorkes from a farmer on
the estate in lieu of rent.

Georgian mahogany kneehole dressing-table.

The early eighteenth-century pier-glass and *dressing-
table glass* with walnut frames may have been
supplied to Meller in the 1720s.

THE WHITE BEDROOM

So called after the painted seventeenth-century panelling introduced during the nineteenth century from Little Erddig, a manor house added to the estate in 1807 and partly burnt down in 1886.

PICTURES

The walls are hung with a variety of eighteenth- and nineteenth-century topographical prints and watercolours, notably a pen and ink drawing of the east front of Erddig of about 1730.

SAMUEL PROUT (1783–1852)
A View in a Continental Town
Possibly a view of Rouen.
Watercolour

JOHN DOWNMAN, ARA (1750–1824)
General Richard England
Watercolour
Signed and dated 1805
Veteran of the American War of Independence, Lieutenant-Governor of Plymouth, and one of the first colonists of western Upper Canada. Downman was born in nearby Ruabon and specialised in portraits of this kind in chalk and wash.

FURNITURE

The Chippendale period mahogany four-poster bed still retains some of its mid-nineteenth-century bed-hangings: a printed cotton chintz of naturally drawn flower sprays of 1860, similar to a series sold by Hindley & Sons and printed at Bannister Hall in Preston. The other chintz covering the day-bed, armchair and curtains was introduced by the National Trust in 1976.

BETWEEN WINDOWS:

The English walnut bureau cabinet, with the upper section enclosing panels of mirror glass, is possibly the piece supplied to Meller by John Pardoe for £10 5s, mentioned in a payment of 1716–17.

THE SOUTH LANDING

PICTURES

MOSES GRIFFITH (1747–1819)
Four watercolours:
A View of Coed Coch, near Abergele
The seat of J. Lloyd Wynne, a kinsman of Philip Yorke I's second wife.

A View of Coed Coch, near Abergele

A View of the West Front of Erddig from the Park; by Moses Griffith (South Landing)

A View of Teyrdan Hall
The family home of Margaret Holland, who married Simon Yorke II.

A View of the West Front of Erddig from the Park

BRITISH, late seventeenth-century
Reputed Portrait of Tony Leigh in the character of Dominic in 'The Spanish Friar'
Leigh was a gentleman actor, active from 1672 until his death in 1692. But the identification seems no older than the early nineteenth-century inscription, and this may simply be a piece of anti-clerical satire.

VENETIAN, c.1700
Cimon and Pero (Roman Charity)
A popular exemplar of filial piety: Cimon, an aged prisoner awaiting execution, is fed by his daughter Pero, who offers him her breast. Perhaps after Sebastiano Ricci (1659–1734).

FURNITURE

The English seventeenth-century black japanned longcase clock with chinoiserie decoration is signed 'William Andrews, London' and is mentioned in John Meller's cash book of 1709–11.

RIGHT OF DOOR TO LONG GALLERY:

An eighteenth-century triangular lantern case for candle lighting. The glass bell above protects the ceiling from smoke.

CERAMICS

The Bow figure of 'Liberty' by the Muses modeller in the Meissen style, c.1755. This figure can be associated with Thomas Frye, one of the founders of the Bow factory in 1744. Mezzotints by Frye hang in the Blue Bedroom.

THE ATTICS

The staircase leading to the attics is hung with a variety of eighteenth- and nineteenth-century engravings, notably *The Riot in Broad Street, 7th June 1780*, after Francis Wheatley, which includes the figure of Sir Barnard Turner, from whom Louisa Yorke was descended (see p.70). On the Attic Landing itself are photographs of servants taken between 1887 and 1912. Each is accompanied by verses written by Philip Yorke II.

This floor contains nine rooms which housed fifteen beds in the early eighteenth century. In addition, some of John Meller's servants slept on the first floor either in rooms adjacent to the principal bedrooms or in the passages. The attic floor was occupied by the female staff including the housekeeper, until a suite of rooms was set up for her at the south end of the house; male staff slept in quarters in the stables and outhouses.

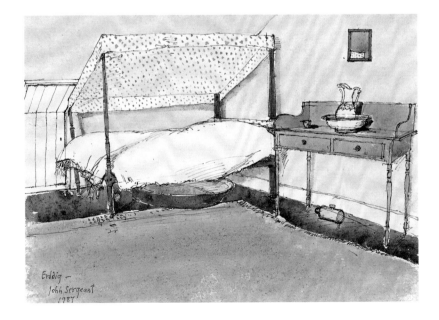

The four-poster bed in the Fire Attic; by John Sergeant, 1987

FURNITURE

Much of the original eighteenth-century furniture was disposed of in the nineteenth century. The rooms were later furnished and decorated with items no longer required by the family.

THE FIRE ATTIC

To the right at the top of the stairs is the Fire Attic, so named after a fire which broke out in the roof above in 1907. It was occupied by Alice Jones, head laundry maid, in the early part of this century.

FURNITURE

The four-poster servant's bed with sloping canopy, designed to fit under the eaves, is similar to those made by Gillow of Lancaster in the late eighteenth century. The feather mattress is supported by sacking strung from the frame with cords and kept in place with a covered wooden headboard.

TEXTILES

The rug is a rare Scottish or 'Kidderminster' carpet, *c.*1800, made up of narrow widths joined together. Few such rugs have survived because inexpensive textiles in everyday use usually wear out and are then discarded.

THE CLOCK ATTIC

The room beyond, known as the Clock Attic, is shown as a sitting-room. Here the housemaids would spend the afternoons working together, sewing and mending until tea-time at four o'clock. This was Matilda 'Tillie' Boulter's bedroom when she was head housemaid in the early 1900s. She spent most of her free time practising the violin and occasionally joined Louisa Yorke's father, the Rev. Thomas Scott, in playing duets.

THE ATTIC BEDROOM

The room on the left at the top of the stairs was shared by Bessie Gittins, engaged in 1909 as nursery maid, and Edith Haycock, second housemaid. By 1911, at her own request, Bessie had left the Nursery to become third housemaid. The bedroom is simply furnished with two iron bedsteads, which were

considered more hygienic than wooden ones. The screens provided a modicum of privacy. No gas or electricity were installed by the Yorkes, lighting being provided by oil lamps and candles.

THE WEST ROOM
(NURSERY)

In the 1720s this was known as 'Ye Worked [ie needlework] Room', and was furnished with a bed lined with green satin, and with a quilted green counterpane, walnut chairs and a black japanned cabinet and chest. Later called the West Room, it is now shown as a nursery.

TOYS

ON SOUTH WALL:

The doll's-house of four rooms was adapted during the nineteenth century from an early eighteenth-century oak cupboard on a stand. Much of the furnishings dates from 1840–80, including the Waltershausen furniture and some homemade pieces, notably the embroidered satin curtains made from a waistcoat given to Simon III on his coming-of-age in 1832. The inscription 'Waste Not Want Not' imitates that painted above the arches of the New Kitchen.

The white teddy bear, dressed in the clothes of Philip Yorke III, and the elephant, both seated in the Victorian wheelbarrow pram, date from about 1900.

The wooden Noah's Ark was made in Germany and given to Simon Yorke IV on his fifth birthday in 1908. There were originally 300 animals and eight people in the set.

The wooden train, comprising engine and three wagons, was also made for Simon's fifth birthday by the estate foreman, William Gittins.

The Regency rocking horse was used by Philip Yorke III.

PICTURES

GILBERT BALDRY
Simon IV (1903–66) and Philip III (1905–78) Yorke as children
Sons of Philip Yorke II by his second wife, Louisa Scott; the last of the Yorkes of Erddig. Numerous other photographs of them are hung here.

The nineteenth-century shower in the Bathroom

THE BATHROOM

This room probably served as a servant's bed-chamber for the West Room until the introduction of plumbing at the end of the nineteenth century. Prior to this, bathing was undertaken in hip-baths set up in front of bedroom fires. In the eighteenth century the family had bathed in cold water in the Bath House sited in the park.

The nineteenth-century portable shower worked by releasing hot water from the cylindrical tank above, supported on pipes painted to imitate bamboo. The water was then recirculated by use of the hand-pump. It was still very much in use in the last Philip Yorke's day.

PICTURES

The walls are hung with mainly maritime prints and watercolours, including one which shows the shower in action.

THE GALLERY

The only room to run from east to west across the full depth of the house, the Gallery has changed little since the late seventeenth century, when Joshua Edisbury commissioned a local carpenter, Philip Rogers of Eyton, to undertake joinery work at Erddig. Rogers probably installed the oak panelling, which would originally have been painted or grained; it was varnished in the nineteenth century.

Intended as a place for both recreation and con-templation, long galleries were traditionally used during inclement weather as a place for exercise and later on as picture galleries, usually for the display of family portraits.

Until the creation of the State Bedroom in the late eighteenth century, the Gallery was the most important room on the first floor.

PICTURES

In 1732 Loveday recorded that the Gallery was 'hung with ye Sibylls, all lengths'. These pictures acquired by Meller and representing divinatory priestesses of Apollo were sold in 1787. In the same year, shortly after the death of his mother, Dorothy (née Hutton), Philip Yorke I introduced the present seventeenth-century portraits inherited from the Hutton family and originally hung in the Yorke's London house in Park Lane.

NORTH WALL (LEFT-HAND SIDE):

After MICHIEL MIEREVELDT (1567–1641)
Elizabeth, Queen of Bohemia (1596–1662)
Panel
Daughter of James I, married Frederick of Bohemia in 1613.

After MICHIEL MIEREVELDT (1567–1641)
Prince Maurice of Orange-Nassau (1567–1625)
Panel
Not, as labelled, Frederick V, King of Bohemia, but the second son of William the Silent and the outstanding military commander of his time.

JACOB FRANSZ. VAN DER MERCK (c.1610–64)
Major Henry Meoles
Panel
Signed and dated 1649
In 1658 he received his commission in William Killigrew's regiment, which had served in the Dutch army during the Thirty Years War.

After DAVID TENIERS the Younger (1610–90)
Dutch Woman Pouring Water
Panel

After FERDINAND VAN KESSEL (1648–96)
Monkey Barbers
Panel

DUTCH, c.1640
King Gustavus Adolphus II (1594–1632)
Warrior king of Sweden, 1611–32.

NORTH WALL (RIGHT-HAND SIDE):

JACOB FRANSZ. VAN DER MERCK (c.1610–64)
Captain Meoles
Panel
Signed and dated 1649
Not, as labelled, Robert Bertie, 1st Earl of Lindsey
(1582–1642), but the son of Major Meoles (above).

Manner of DAVID TENIERS the Younger (1610–90)
Cat Musicians
Panel

BRITISH
A Woman at a window

After CORNELIUS JOHNSON (1593–1664)
Thomas Coventry, 1st Lord Coventry (1578–1640)
In his robes as Lord Keeper of the Great Seal, the
purse of office over his left shoulder.

Manner of CORNELIUS JOHNSON (1593–1664)
An Unknown Woman
Panel
Inscribed: *Anno 162[?6]/Aetatis [?]*

BRITISH, 161[?]
An Unknown Woman
Panel

BRITISH, ? early seventeenth-century
Sir Thomas Egerton, Viscount Brackley
(1540–1616/17)
Panel
Lord Chancellor, 1603–16/17.

SOUTH WALL (LEFT-HAND SIDE):

JOHN SHACKLETON (active 1742–67)
Thomas Kinaston (d.1752)
Signed and dated 173[?]
Second son of William and Jane Kinaston of Ruyton
Hall, Shropshire.

? Sir JOSHUA REYNOLDS, PRA (1723–92)
Edward Kinaston (d.1792)
The grandson of William and Jane Kinaston,

painted in 1760. His daughter Margaret left these
family portraits to the Yorkes, who were cousins.

After DAVID TENIERS the Younger (1610–90)
A Cordial Seller
Panel
The original (*Autumn* from a set of the Four
Seasons) is in the National Gallery.

Manner of MARCUS GHEERAERTS the Younger
(1561/2–1635)
An Unknown Woman
Panel
Inscribed: *An[n]i 1629/AEta suae. 41*

Attributed to MICHIEL MIEREVELDT (1567–1641)
Supposed portrait of the Duke of Buckingham
Panel

BETTY RATCLIFFE (c.1735–c.1810) after ANTHONY
VAN DYCK (1599–1641)
Sir Kenelm Digby (1603–65) and his Family
Drawing
According to a label on the back, copied in 1766.

BETTY RATCLIFFE (c.1735–c.1810)
View of Conway Castle, 1782
Coloured chalks

SOUTH WALL (RIGHT-HAND SIDE):

After J. A. RAVESTEYN (c.1570–1657)
Prince Frederick Henry, Crown Prince Palatine
(1614–29)
Panel
Inscribed as painted in 1623
The eldest son of Frederick V of the Palatinate, King
of Bohemia, and Princess Elizabeth, 'the Winter
Queen', daughter of James I.

BETTY RATCLIFFE (c.1735–c.1810) after HUBERT
DROUAIS the Younger (1699–1767)
The Sons of the Duc de Bouillon as Montagnards
According to a label on the back, copied from a
print in 1765. The original picture is in the Frick
Collection, New York.

DUTCH, 1629
An Unknown Boy with a Bird
Panel
Said to be a child of the Winter Queen of Bohemia.
If so, Prince Edward (1625–63).

JOSEPH ALLEN (1769–1839) after ? ADRIAEN VAN
CRONENBURGH (1520/5–1604), 1568
Catherine of Berain (1534/5–91)
Granddaughter of an illegitimate son of Henry VII,

painted as the wife of Sir Richard Clough, an immensely rich merchant and partner of Sir Thomas Gresham, builder of the first house at Osterley (also NT). The original is in the National Museum of Wales, Cardiff.

MARCUS GHEERAERTS the Younger (1561/2–1635)
An Unknown Man (b.1592/3)
Panel
Inscribed: *Aetatis Suae 35./Anno Do.1628* and (under a vetch) *Humilior Melior*
Might *Melior* be a pun on Meller, and this be an early member of that family?

After DAVID TENIERS the Younger (1610–90)
A Gardener and his Wife
Panel

BRITISH, c.1630?
An Unknown Man, known as 'Lord Arundel'
Possibly a later pastiche.

MODELS

The models were made by Elizabeth Ratcliffe (c.1735–c.1810), daughter of a Chester clockmaker and known to the Yorkes as 'Betty the little'. She was lady's maid and companion to Mrs Dorothy Yorke, mother of Philip Yorke I. The Yorkes, recognising their protégée's talent, paid for her education and encouraged her artistic development.

The Chinese Pagoda

The pagoda was made in 1767 and is based on an engraving of 'The Great Pagoda as first intended' in William Chambers's *Gardens and Buildings at Kew* (1763). Betty Ratcliffe adapted the design, however, altering the scale from ten to six storeys and elaborating the details, particularly of the varied fretwork rails surrounding each storey. She also added the small bells, which were not a feature of Chambers's design.

The model has a wooden base but most of it is constructed of vellum, to which crushed mica, slivers of mother-of-pearl, and fragments of coloured glass are glued. The carved and painted wooden stand on which the model sits is an outstanding piece of chinoiserie furniture, possibly made by John Linnell (d.1796) of Berkeley Square, London. It retains the original green, white and silvered colouring.

The Ruins of the Temple of the Sun at Palmyra

The Ruins were made in 1773 and also have an architectural publication as their source: Robert Wood's *The Ruins of Palmyra* (1753). No particular view was copied and Betty Ratcliffe adapted the Neo-classical design, treating her source material in a rather arbitrary and romantic manner: for example, she added the delicately trailing vegetation. Like the Chinese Pagoda, the Ruins are constructed of mother-of-pearl, mica and glass fragments.

The carved gilt and glazed case, also in a Neo-classical style, was probably supplied by Thomas Fentham, carver, gilder and picture-frame maker of The Strand, London. The design of the frieze is almost identical to that which appears on a frame supplied by Fentham in the 1770s for the portrait of Simon and Etheldred Yorke (now in the Chinese Room). A payment of £15 12s 6d to him in 1775 may have been for the case.

The smaller model of an exotic bird perched among flowers was also made of mother-of-pearl and other materials. Like the larger models, it was made by Betty Ratcliffe at the Yorkes' London house in Park Lane, and on the death of Dorothy Yorke in 1787, it survived the perilous journey to Erddig.

FURNITURE

The appearance of the Gallery would originally have been much less cluttered. During the eighteenth-century refashioning of the ground-floor rooms and the removal of items from the Yorkes' London house, more furniture was placed here.

The seven walnut chairs are mentioned in the 1726 inventory. Four of them came from John Meller's Saloon and were originally covered in caffoy – a cut-wool velvet of brilliant yellow and deep crimson. They were much admired by the antiquarian John Loveday in 1732. Two of these, still with their original covers, flank the door from the Landing, whilst the others have maroon case covers c.1905.

FLANKING DOOR TO NORTH LANDING:

The semicircular carved and gilt pier-tables were probably made by Thomas Fentham, c.1778, as the decoration is identical to that found on the stand for the model of the Ruins of Palmyra. The tops made by Betty Ratcliffe in 1778 consist of small fragments of mother-of-pearl arranged to depict Chinese landscapes surrounded by a rococo floral border.

ON LEFT:

An eighteenth-century black japanned bureau cabinet bearing the stamp 'R.F.' and identical in form to the scarlet japanned cabinet in the State Bedroom. Both may have been supplied to Meller by Belchier in the

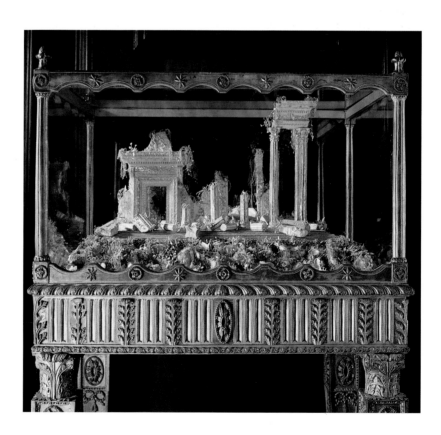

The Ruins of the Temple of the Sun at Palmyra; model by Betty Ratcliffe, 1773 (Gallery)

1720s. The mirrored door panels have been re-moved and the inner japanned panels reversed.

The Morocco leather-bound travelling trunk came to Erddig in 1770 as the linen-press of Elizabeth Yorke, according to Louisa Yorke's *Facts and Fancies*.

AT FAR RIGHT END OF GALLERY:

The James II walnut day-bed and three stools were said by Louisa Yorke to have come from the Yorkes' Park Lane house although Meller's 1726 inventory records a large quantity of caned furniture in the Gallery. The bed and largest stool once had caffoy loose covers. The two windows were also hung with caffoy pelmets in the early twentieth century but these are now too fragile to be shown.

MISCELLANEOUS

The sedan chair was, according to Louisa Yorke, used by Margaret Yorke, wife of Simon II.

She would get into the Sedan Chair in the Lower Hall . . . the footman would carry their mistress, well tucked in with all the windows shut and the curtains drawn (air was not appreciated in her day!) and the door would not be opened until she arrived at her destination, inside the house of her friend.

The chair was rediscovered in an outhouse in 1903 and restored by Edward Davies of Chester.

The mid-eighteenth-century mahogany-framed exercise stool, known as a chamber horse, was used to simulate horse-riding. According to Louisa Yorke, it was given by a member of the family and delivered by canal to Chester.

The Victorian beechwood double rocking chair, known as a nursery yacht, has caned seats and a carpeted base. It was made in Colwyn Bay by John Hughes.

The Bagatelle board is Regency and was made by F. C. Lynn of Liverpool. It retains its original cues, balls, brass pegs and hoops and score sheets.

DOCUMENTS

The vellum Elizabethan charter is a land grant: in 1580 the Erddig township was granted to Dr John Yale, great-uncle of Elihu Yale, the neighbour of Joshua Edisbury at Plas Grono.

The parchment lists the names of all the sheriffs in Denbighshire.

The North Landing. The blue glass bottles hanging on the walls are early fire extinguishers

THE NORTH LANDING

The landing for the main staircase of the house with the most important bedchambers leading from it.

PICTURES

JOSEPH ALLEN (1769–1839)
Diana Wynne, Mrs Philip Yorke (d.1805) *as a Widow*
Daughter and heiress of Piers Wynne of Dyffryn Aled, she married Philip Yorke I, as his second wife, in 1782. A somewhat improvident, scatter-brained, but amiable woman.

JOSEPH ALLEN (1769–1839)
? *Piers Wynne Yorke* (1784–1837) *as a Boy*
Probably the first son of Philip Yorke I and his second wife, Diana Wynne of Dyffryn Aled.

FRANCIS WHEATLEY (1747–1801)
Sir Barnard Turner (1736–84)
Signed and dated 1783
Louisa Yorke, mother of Simon IV and Philip III, was a descendant of Sir Barnard, who was MP for Suffolk and Sheriff of the City of London. The sword he holds is supposed to be that in the case below, although the hilt is quite different.

FURNITURE

The curiously ugly nineteenth-century pier-tables, with shaped tops covered in crimson velvet and with turned and foliated legs, were constructed from curtain poles, probably supplied by Gillows in the 1820s and adapted later in the century. Louisa Yorke records that until 1902, when she put them here, they were covered in muslin draperies and used in some of the bedrooms.

CLOCK

The early eighteenth-century longcase clock with arched dial is signed 'Jno. Ratcliffe, Chester'. The japanned case with domed hood and carved flambeaux finials was probably made in London. John Ratcliffe was father of Betty Ratcliffe.

BELLS

The hand bells, of which there were originally eight in the set, were given to Louisa Yorke by her uncle Edward Scott in 1885. She used them to teach the bell ringers of Marksbury to ring changes and tunes.

METALWORK

The English small sword of 1760–1, the silver hilt bearing the mark of John Rowe, was presented by the Duke of York to Barnard Turner in 1761.

THE STATE BEDROOM

Following Philip Yorke I's marriage to Elizabeth Cust in 1770, the State Bed, previously in the Best Bedchamber (now the Dining Room), was moved to the first floor, as it was no longer fashionable to have bedrooms on the ground floor. The room was redecorated with a hand-painted Chinese wallpaper depicting flowering trees and shrubs with a profusion of birds, butterflies and small insects, set against a rich green-blue background. The chimneypiece, probably by John Devall, was introduced at the same period.

Subsidence, due to coal-mining, caused extensive damage to the structure of the house and by 1968 rainwater poured through the ceiling of this room. This affected the furniture, particularly the State Bed and the wallpaper, which was peeling off in many places. When the National Trust took over in the 1970s, the wallpaper was carefully removed and conserved. It was rehung in 1977.

STATE BED

The State Bed is a rare surviving example of a *lit à la duchesse*, a style of bed introduced at the end of the seventeenth century by the Anglo-Dutch architect Daniel Marot (1661–1752), who came to England in the service of William of Orange. The tester (canopy) extends the entire length of the bed and is suspended on chains from the ceiling, rather than being supported by foot posts.

On 17 April 1720 Simon Yorke I reported to John Meller that he had called on 'Mr Hurt ... to press his sending ye bed he is making on Monday next'. The craftsman's wife informed him that 'ye bed as to their worke hath been finished, but ye gilding and carving is not ready'. Mr Hurt was probably John Hutt, a cabinetmaker in St Paul's Churchyard, London. The carved and gilded ornament is so close to that found on the glasses supplied by Belchier that he was probably responsible for some elements of the embellishments.

The bed-hangings, including the cornice, valances and the counterpane, are made of a number of different pieces of embroidered silk, which in many areas are fixed with glue directly on to the oak structure. The silk is embroidered in the Chinese manner known as 'Indian needlework' and was originally a shimmering white with brilliant, almost gaudy, coloured embroidery. Such fabrics were imported to England in the early eighteenth century by the East India Company: Meller may have bought them directly from London or alternatively acquired them from his neighbour Elihu Yale of Plas Grono, who until 1699 traded for the Company. Louisa Yorke recorded in 1923 that the bed-hangings were repaired by Walford & Spokes of Oxford about 1900, using fabric from the window curtains; again in 1906 worn pieces were copied by the Ladies Needlework Guild.

The underside of the tester is decorated with a flock of birds and in the centre hovers a large embroidered peacock, set against a gilded strapwork background. Two other peacocks occupy the corners at the foot of the bed. Each bird is cut from a piece of embroidered silk and mounted on to a shaped wooden block. The curved headboard is also elaborately decorated with a carved cartouche

The State Bedroom

containing a peacock at the top, and at the base with two gilded hawks' heads, which are probably the work of Belchier.

By 1968 the bed was in a severe state of deterioration: Philip Yorke III allowed it to be removed to the Victoria & Albert Museum, where it was painstakingly conserved over two years. The Museum generously agreed to its return in 1977, but insisted on the glass screen to protect it.

OTHER FURNITURE

ON RIGHT:

The English scarlet japanned bureau cabinet was probably bought from Belchier by Meller in the 1720s. It bears a stamp 'R.F.', similar to that found on the

black japanned cabinet of identical form in the Gallery. The cabinet was listed as being in the 'Blew Mohair Room' in the 1726 inventory. It was moved here from the Gallery in the 1970s. Despite the light damage to the exterior, when opened, it reveals the spectacularly bright original colouring.

The exceptionally rare English green japanned side-chairs and two oval stools were acquired by 1726, probably from Belchier. They are listed in the inventory for that year as being in the Best Bedchamber and as having gold stuff covers. These would have been slip covers made of the same embroidered silk as the bed. Although these no longer exist, the original undercovers of blue-green worsted, are a rare survival. The material is impressed with an overall pattern of sinuous lines. The chairs appear to have been well used by the Yorkes. By 1906 Louisa Yorke recorded that they had become very shabby and so were sent for repair to Edward Davies in Chester. Two had been placed in the Blue Bedroom and painted brown to complement the panelling there; a third, also painted, had been upholstered with embroidery worked by Victoria Yorke and placed in the Chapel. The two from the Blue Bedroom were restored in 1907 and returned to the State Bedroom. However, the third remains in the Chapel.

TO LEFT OF BED:

The Coromandel lacquered screen is Chinese. It is one of the few pieces at Erddig thought to have belonged to Joshua Edisbury. It is described in a letter of 1682 from Elihu Yale, who was then Governor of Fort St George in India, as a 'Japan Skreen', which he intended to send on the 'Bengall Merchant' ship as a gift for Edisbury's wife. In a postscript Yale advised Edisbury that 'since the foregoing 'tis my misfortune not to prevail with the captain to carry the skreenes, his ship being full already, so pray excuse me 'til next yeare'. Louisa Yorke recorded that the screen was used for many years in the Dining Room. It was placed here in 1902 and was repaired by Edward Davies two years later.

Its six panels depict a continuous design: on one side travellers, hunters and soldiers in a mountainous landscape; and on the other a scene of exotic birds and waterfowl set in a mountainous riverscape.

The three eighteenth-century pier-glasses may be the work of John Belchier.

The pair of black japanned chests decorated with chinoiserie motifs and on wooden stands is eighteenth-century.

FLOWER PIECES AND EMBROIDERIES

The arrangement of flowers, made of silk, paper, wire and wool mounted on a silk background, was created by Betty Ratcliffe in 1775. The carved oval frame was probably supplied by Fentham. It is likely that he also supplied frames for the three flower embroideries of about 1773, also made by her.

The two modern silk flower arrangements were made by Lucy Askew in 1986.

(Right) A mezzotint self-portrait by Thomas Frye, 1760 (Blue Bedroom)

THE BLUE BEDROOM

During the late eighteenth-century reorganisation of the house by Philip Yorke I and his wife Elizabeth, this room was rearranged to accommodate the bed from the Second Best Bedchamber (now the Tapestry Room) on the ground floor.

PICTURES

THOMAS FRYE (1710–62)
Part of two sets of mezzotints, published in 1760 and 1761–2. Although the man holding an engraving tool is thought to be Frye himself, the others were probably not intended to be straightforward portraits, but were exercises in dramatic poses, with Frye's artist and actor friends as models.

FURNITURE

The early eighteenth-century bed is a *lit à la duchesse* type, similar to, but less opulent than, the State Bed. In the late eighteenth to early nineteenth century it was reupholstered in blue silk and wool damask, although traces of the original crimson damask have been found adhering to the top of the tester.

BETWEEN WINDOWS:

The early eighteenth-century giltwood pier-glass was made by Belchier *c.*1720. A section of the embellishment at the bottom of the frame is now lost.

BELOW:

The mahogany chest-of-drawers with boldly gadrooned top and carved bracket feet may have been supplied by John Cobb in 1770.

ON LEFT:

A late Georgian mahogany clothes press. The mahogany dressing glass on it is *c.*1830.

RIGHT OF BED:

The washstand is Victorian.

TEXTILES

The carpet is English, *c.*1900.

THE INNER HALL
(NORTH)

At the bottom of the main stairs and those leading to the lower ground floor, the walls are covered with a series of illuminated addresses presented to members of the Yorke family. These include one to Philip Yorke II from the management, colliers and workmen of the Bryn-yr-Owen colliery on his coming-of-age in 1870. Another from the Mayor, Aldermen and Burgesses of the town of Wrexham was given on his second marriage in 1902. Another to Simon Yorke IV was presented by the tenants of the Erddig estate on his coming-of-age in 1924.

THE FAILURES GALLERY

Used as the entrance to the Chapel by the servants attending daily prayers, the Yorkes named this the Failures Gallery because of the various gifts and objects displayed here, which for one reason or another were not considered worthy of show elsewhere in the house.

PICTURES

The range of small oils, watercolours and prints includes a portrait of Philip Yorke II as Mayor of Wrexham in 1897.

FURNITURE

The carved oak hall seat, settle and side-table are all nineteenth-century and are traditionally associated with General John Yorke, brother of Simon Yorke III, who lived at Plas Newydd, Llangollen (see p.23).

CLOCK

The George III longcase clock has a brass and silvered dial signed 'Jno. Ratcliffe, Wrexham'.

STATUETTES

A selection of Parian ware, alabaster and plaster casts, including the figures of Venus, Hebe, Bacchus and Ariadne together with copies of Thorwaldson sculpture bought by the Yorkes in Copenhagen.

MUSICAL INSTRUMENTS

The mid-nineteenth-century harmonium in a rosewood case is attributed to H. Christophe & Etienne.

THE CHAPEL

The Chapel occupies the far end of the north wing added by Meller in the 1720s. In 1732 Loveday noted, 'The Chappel is not quite finished ye pews &c. of Oak'.

The present arrangement reflects the Chapel's appearance during the late nineteenth and early twentieth centuries, when rich stencilling on lining paper was introduced, including the deep border of lilies of about 1907–9. The family pew on the right was entered via the Chinese Room. Servants sat in the pews to the left. The metal ceiling was added as a fire precaution in 1908.

STAINED GLASS

Two windows, incorporating fragments of fifteenth-century French glass, were brought in 1909 from Wimpole Hall, Cambridgeshire, home of the Yorkes' kinsmen, the Earls of Hardwicke. The third window is eighteenth-century by William Price.

FRIEZE

The biblical text running just below the ceiling was cut out by Philip Yorke II in 1909 with the assistance of his elder son, and was put up in celebration of his

The Chapel

two sons' births – Simon in 1903 and Philip in 1905. Both children were baptised here, though today the Chapel is unconsecrated.

PICTURES

After CARLO MARATTA (1625–1713)
Madonna and Child with Angels
A variant copy of Maratta's *Nativity* in the Dresden Gallery.

ALTARPIECE:

BRITISH, eighteenth-century
Madonna and Child
Somewhat reminiscent of the studies of Madonnas, and Mothers and Children, that Benjamin West and Richard Cosway did *c.*1760–70.

After GUIDO RENI (1575–1642)
Adoration of the Shepherds
Poor, probably English, copy of the octagonal picture in the Pushkin Museum, Moscow. It reverses the original, and so was probably painted from an engraving.

FLEMISH, early seventeenth-century
Madonna and Child in a Landscape
Copper

FURNISHINGS

The carved oak reredos of 1663 is surmounted by a Victorian carved border bought at a sale in 1909. The altar cloth was embroidered in 1855 by the Hon. Elizabeth Cust and her sister Lucy, aunts of Victoria Yorke (née Cust). The red plush cushions are early nineteenth-century. The palms of 1892 and 1898 were given to Simon and Victoria Yorke.

The plain crucifix was made by William Gittins, the estate carpenter, *c.*1898.

The white marble statue of the Virgin of the Immaculate Conception was given to Simon and Victoria Yorke in 1846 as a wedding present by Simon's brother-in-law, Charles Birch Reynardson, and placed in the Chapel in 1914.

The oak lectern was carved by John Davies of Wrexham in 1858.

The Gothic carved oak prayer desk was bought by Philip Yorke II in 1895 from the sale of Leasowe Castle, Cheshire, the home of his grandfather, Sir Edward Cust.

The hatchment to Simon Yorke II (d.1834) was set up here in 1836.

ORGAN

The American organ and the organ case are entirely independent of one another. According to Louisa Yorke, the organ, made by W. Bell & Co. of Guelph, Ontario, was given by Victoria Yorke and her son Philip to Esclusham church in 1880. In 1895 it was removed to the Chapel when the church acquired a larger pipe organ. The case, surmounted by an elaborate broken cornice, was, according to the same source, acquired in 1913 from the church at Worthenbury, south-east of Wrexham.

PICTURE

ON LEFT-HAND WALL OUTSIDE TRIBES ROOM:

THOMAS BADESLADE (*c.*1715–50)
The Garden and Park at Erddig in 1739
Pencil
Engraved by W. H. Toms and published the same year. It clearly illustrates the formal planting and

canal on the east front and the rides through the park to the north. The house is shown with its original cupola, forecourt gates and screens, all now lost.

THE TRIBES ROOM

This room is named after Philip Yorke I's book *The Royal Tribes of Wales* (1799). The walls are decorated with the coats of arms of the noble Welsh families illustrated in it.

OVER FIREPLACE:

A panel incorporating the arms of the Yorkes, together with those of families into which they married: Hutton, Cust, Wynne, Holland, Cust, Puleston and Scott. The eighth panel was left blank, as both Simon IV and Philip III were bachelors.

FLANKING FIREPLACE:

The pair of glass armorial panels depicts the arms of Meller (1713) and Yorke (1771).

In the eighteenth century the room was used as a billiard-room, although it also appears to have provided a secondary access out to the west front. By the nineteenth century it was used as an entrance, when the draughty ground-floor Entrance Hall became rather more of a music room.

FURNITURE

The six Georgian walnut hall-chairs with waisted backs are decorated with the Yorke crest.

SCULPTURE

CHRISTOPHER MOORE (1790–1863)
Sir Charles Cust
Plaster; dated 1832
In the early twentieth century it was in the Library.

THE GARDEN MUSEUM

The Museum houses a small exhibition about the history and the evolution of the garden at Erddig and a selection of garden implements.

TOOLS

A late nineteenth-century potato grading fork and a carved garden fork.

A metal leaf sweeper made in Pennsylvania and a stone and wrought-iron garden roller.

An early twentieth-century lawn edger.

A wooden strickle, used for sharpening scythes.

A wood and iron fruit gatherer and a wood and metal currant picker.

A pair of terracotta forcing or blanching pots and a selection of other terracotta plant pots.

Two glass propagation bells and two cast-iron lantern cloches.

A series of zinc and tin plant labels, including those for varieties of plums, pears, apples and greengages grown as espaliers along the garden walls.

The canal in the garden was regularly used by the Yorkes for boating and skating. The model boats and barge are late nineteenth- and early twentieth-century. The leather boots with ice skates screwed into the soles are Edwardian.

THE FAMILY MUSEUM

This contains a miscellany of ethnographic and natural history specimens collected by the Yorkes: shells; a hornets' nest; skulls; rocks and spears. All are jumbled together in a display case which was probably made by one of the Erddig joiners.

The Family Museum

CHAPTER SEVEN
THE PARK AND GARDENS

There has been a park at Erddig since medieval times when 'Park Glyn', one of the five major parks within the Lordship of Bromfield and Yale, extended over a thousand or more acres of the Clywedog valley and adjacent lands, north of the present house. As well as providing hunting and venison for the Lord's table, enclosed woodland within the park, growing on the steep valley sides of the Afon Clywedog's flood plain, was cropped for timber and especially for its underwood. The latter was converted to charcoal for smelting lead, an activity sometimes carried out within the park itself.

By the end of the sixteenth century, the park had been enclosed for agricultural purposes and was farmed by tenants, although it still retained former areas of enclosed woodland. It also had a pair of water-mills powered by a leat from the Afon Clywedog. Among those who owned land adjoining the park at that time was one 'John Erthig'.

'Erthig' (or its many variants) is known as a place name from the early fourteenth century, but it wasn't until the mid-sixteenth century that it began to appear as a family surname. This association of family and place was short-lived, however, as the

The Victorian Garden

*The canal and formal
garden to the east of
the house, c.1730*

estate was sold in 1595 to David Yale of Tattenhall for 'two hundred, four-score and tenne poundes of lawfull money of England'. Dr Yale, later described as 'of Erthigge' (although the family name is more usually associated with the nearby Plas Grono), also held lands in Glyn Park as well as the water-mills there. Eventually however, the lease of Erddig was acquired by John Edisbury of Pentre-y-Clawdd, who willed it to his eldest son Joshua.

Joshua Edisbury seems to have been an able and knowledgeable gardener and began laying out his gardens soon after work began on the house. In 1685, he contracted Philip Rogers of Eaton, a carpenter who was also engaged separately to carry out works to the house, to 'doe all ye Carpenter's work for two banqueting houses to be erected at Erthigg'. These faced each other at the northern and southern ends of a broad terrace walk which ran the width of Edisbury's new gardens. A grassed court was laid out to the east front of the house, with the kitchen garden to the south and a 'Harty Choake Garden' to the north, where it could be supplied with manure from the adjacent Cow Yard. Steps descending from the Terrace Walk led on to a central axis walk through the 'Best Garden', which was laid out in two quartered

designs to north and south. Beyond its walls lay the twin orchards, separated by the central 'Fir Walk' which led to the eastern boundary of the gardens.

Each garden was enclosed by walls, on which was grown a wide variety of pears, plums, green-gages, nectarines, peaches, apricots, cherries and grapes, not to mention fruit growing in the orchards themselves. Letters written in the early 1690s to Joshua Edisbury in London describe 'diging the borders' in the orchard, the raising of melons in hot-beds (in long-vanished greenhouses), the grafting of fruit trees and the planting of peas, beans and 'collyflour' seeds.

Once John Meller had formally acquired the estate in 1716, he commissioned a thorough survey of all 'Wall Fruit in Erthig Gardens' and immediately set about replacing gaps and planting a 'new wall' with fruit. Entries in the accounts at that time suggest the creation of a new kitchen garden against the existing south wall of the gardens and considerable other changes in the gardens. Letters to John Meller from his steward at Erddig, Richard Jones, also record the levelling and paving of the front (western) court and the erection of a boundary wall with a formal ironwork gate and screen by Robert and John Davies of Wrexham, weighing some 56 tons and costing £150 11s 6d.

Meller's alterations to the gardens coincided with substantial new works in other parts of the demesne. Payments are recorded in 1718 for 'ffers', and later for the purchase of '140 Yew-trees'; entries concerning the planting of trees in Gwern Erthig, adjacent to a new stone bridge over the Afon Ddu, and the gravelling of a walk there indicate the creation of a formal approach to the house. Meanwhile, works 'at ye Castle walk' and the planting of Hornbeam suggest the creation of an extended pleasure ground in wooded areas north of the house.

An unsigned and undated design for the area east of Edisbury's garden shows a formal, decorative canal aligned on a curved and terraced mount. South of the canal, the plan shows a formal 'wilderness' with a circular lawn at its centre, although there is no evidence that this was ever laid out. North of the canal was a broad, rectangular pond, later called the Menagerie pond, and next to it a trapezoidal pond with a curious arrangement of scalloped hedges at its centre, reminiscent of Renaissance water parterres, as at Wilton. Supplies of lime between November 1721 and June 1722, probably to seal the ponds and prevent leaks, indicate that the canal and ponds were then under construction in the field adjacent to the east side of the gardens. It seems that the canal and ponds were excavated first and only later enclosed within the garden walls, which were then planted with fruit trees. The new gardens appear to have been nearing completion towards the end of 1724, when they first appear as a separate item in the accounts.

Meller's gardens and pleasure grounds are shown in an engraved bird's-eye view by Thomas Badeslade and William Henry Toms, for which Simon Yorke I paid 5 guineas in 1739, some six years after Meller's death. This accurate and detailed view shows the house, with Meller's extensions to Joshua Edisbury's central block, and the west front courtyard with the Davies brothers' gate and

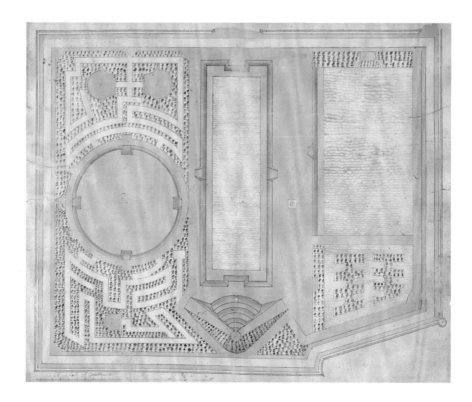

Design for a formal garden at Erddig, attributed to Stephen Switzer, c.1725

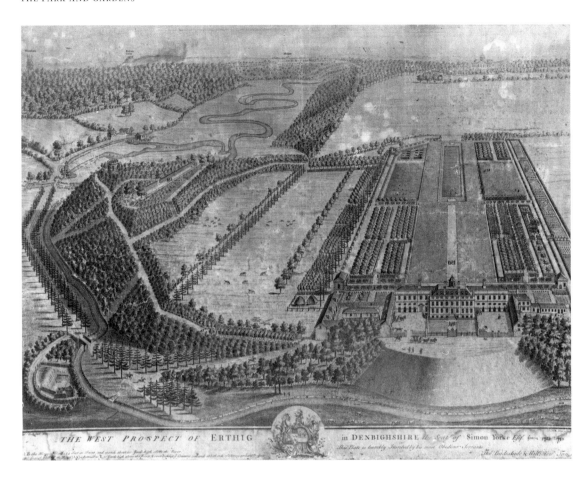

THE WEST PROSPECT OF ERTHIG   in DENBIGHSHIRE the Seat of Simon Yorke Esq

Thomas Badeslade's 1740 bird's-eye view engraving of the house and garden

screen, erected some twenty years earlier. The remains of Edisbury's gardens and orchards are also visible, although much of the latter has been replaced on the south side by a planting of conifers and broadleaf trees.

The central axis of the gardens is shown as a broad gravelled walk leading through an extensive lawn to the canal, at the eastern extremity of which an open *clairvoyée* allowed views to Sontley and beyond. South of the canal, a rectangular bowling green, with a double row of trees at its western end and, to the east, a pair of enclosed formally arranged plantings of trees, balanced the two formal ponds on the north side of the canal. North of the formal gardens was a tree nursery, while to the

south a kitchen garden extended the full length of the wall, with an open 'drying ground' at its western extremity.

The gravel walks laid out by John Meller through areas of ancient woodland, north of Great and Little Castle Fields, are also indicated. In addition, Meller included within his pleasure grounds the ancient motte-and-bailey of Castell-y-Glyn, thereby giving Erddig an added sense of history and continuity. His conversion of the motte itself into a formal mount – a garden feature quite common at that time – by the addition of a spiral path ascending to its summit, was an inspired piece of design.

Throughout the 1740s, Simon Yorke I continued to develop the pleasure grounds in the woodland north of the gardens and added new plantations, probably of Beech. But by the time Philip Yorke I succeeded in 1767, the garden at Erddig would have looked decidedly old-fashioned, though to a man of his antiquarian tastes that would hardly have mattered. He concentrated his resources on 'improvements' to the park, relying on the advice of William Emes. Emes had started out as head gardener at Kedleston in Derbyshire, but subsequently built up a successful landscape practice in the Midlands and Welsh borders. In autumn 1766 he visited Erddig on four occasions and the following year he was again in attendance, charging 8½ guineas for his visits and for a drawing of improvements to areas formerly in Glyn Park between the Wrexham road in the west and the road to Sontley in the east, known by this time as French Mill meadows.

Their main purpose was to control the serious flooding of the meandering Afon Clywedog by the excavation of a new, more direct channel at the southern edge of the valley. His proposals for weirs, cascades and a sinuous riverine lake doubling as a mill pond were costed at around £1,000. In the event a simpler scheme omitting the lake was adopted, although the estimate of £350 for these works by John Caesar, Philip Yorke's steward, proved to be a wild underestimate.

The object of these improvements was primarily concerned with increasing the value of agricultural land and hence, as much of it was let to tenants, the rent which could be charged on it. The skill of professional 'Improvers' such as Emes lay in their ability to achieve this end, while at the same time enhancing the appearance of the landscape, as defined by the aesthetics of the time.

Work began as early as 1768–9 and continued until 1775, although the larger part was completed by 1773. For much of this time, between twenty and thirty men were continually employed under Emes' directions, at a cost of roughly £350 a year. Emes was in attendance at Erddig on a regular basis, but the day-to-day running of works were left to his foreman, one Joseph Bowmer.

At the same time, works were in progress elsewhere in the demesne, with the building of an ice-house and the remodelling by Emes of a small building below Castle Hill as an ornamented Dairy House, with gravelled walks through the surrounding pleasure ground. Primarily decorative, the Dairy House also provided accommodation, for Emes requested its use for a workman: it remained habitable up to the twentieth century.

In January 1775, Emes visited Philip Yorke at Erddig to discuss works beyond those areas first outlined in his original proposals. The levelling and amalgamation of fields was extended southwards along the Afon Ddu from its confluence with the Clywedog, to finish at the Cylindrical Cascade, for which plans were already in hand. These 'improved' lands were then to be enclosed by a hedge. Following the harvest in 1777, the estate workmen became involved in 'building a dam and floodgates' at or near the confluence of the Afon Ddu and the Afon Clywedog: they also cut a new length of mill race in the same year.

In May 1778, Philip Yorke received an 'Estimate and contract for continuing the river on the west side of Erddig to the conflux of the rivulets as submitted by William Emes'. Emes contracted to dig a new channel for the river west of the house between the Cylindrical Cascade in the north and the two tributaries of the Afon Ddu in the south. He also proposed to move some 18,000 tons of soil to create two level terraces within an open pasture, removing some field boundaries, planting trees and extending an existing path.

The remains of these levelled terraces can still be seen on the west side of the river. Emes' men appear to have ceased work at Erddig at the end of 1780, although developments continued for a year or more in the gardens and pleasure grounds. An account of a visit to Erddig, published in 1781, described Emes' landscape on the north side of the park: 'The approach to Erddig, and the well-timbered wood overhanging the banqueting room, which is placed on the edge of a murmuring brook that skirts a large verdant meadow, have a peculiar beauty. The walks thro' the wood and around the banqueting room, are traced out with that taste and elegance, which distinguish the manners of the proprietor.'

Philip Yorke died in 1804 and was succeeded by his son Simon, eldest and only surviving son of his first marriage to Elizabeth Cust. Simon Yorke's contribution to the landscape of Erddig was that of a careful manager rather than as an innovator. The accounts for that period are full of the day-to-day purchases of an efficient and well-maintained household.

The first gardener of whom we have a portrait is Thomas Pritchard, who worked for both Philip I and Simon Yorke II. He was painted in 1830 at the age of 67:

> Our Gardener, old, and run to seed,
> Was once a tall and slender reed . . .
> The Melons raised by Glass and Frame,
> With Cucumbers of various Name,
> The trees he pruned with stubby knife,
> To bear their fruit for longer life.

Pritchard was succeeded in 1841 by James Phillips, who oversaw the first substantial changes in 70 years. In a return to the formality of the early eighteenth century, he laid out L-shaped beds and box hedges on the parterre under the east front. New stalagmite-like fountains were supplied by Blashfields in 1861 as the centrepiece of the design. This firm was based in Grantham and so may have been recommended by Simon Yorke III's relatives at nearby Belton. The cast-iron vases beside the central path and the gates at the end of the Moss Walk were both presents to Simon and Victoria Yorke on their wedding in 1846. Phillips planted roses around the sundial in the north-eastern corner of the garden, but had difficulty with the names:

> Old-fashioned, in his notions, he
> With foreign names, did not agree
> 'Quatre-Saisons' 'Quarter-Sessions' meant,
> The 'Bijou' as the 'By Joe' went,
> 'Glory to die John' was the Rose,
> Which each as 'Gloire de Dijon' knows,
> No Green-house here 'twas his advice
> The Antique Frames would well suffice.

In 1834, Simon Yorke III embarked on an extensive programme of planting in and around Erddig and Sontley demesnes, those in Sontley forming the larger part of what is now known as Forest Wood. By 1844, the central open area of what is now called Big Wood was planted with oak, while Coed-y-Glyn wood was replanted soon after.

In 1854, the Forest Lodge was built 'upon the New Drive to Marchweil'. The earlier plantations here had provided a visual boundary to lands south and east of Erddig, allowing their later conversion to parkland from enclosed fields. The construction of Forest Lodge and the associated drive continued this process and also served to integrate Sontley demesne more fully into the landscape as viewed from Erddig. The drive, which was planted with an 'Ornamental Row of trees', including Wellingtonia, Austrian Pine, Deodar Cedar and Cedar of Lebanon, Douglas Fir and Araucaria, was opened on New Year's Day, 1864.

The gardens also were undergoing development at this time. Among the wedding presents given in 1846 to Simon Yorke and his wife Victoria, daughter of Sir Edward Cust, was a pair of gates from Simon's brother, John. These were installed at the eastern end of the gardens, terminating what became known as the Moss Walk. The 'Terrace Walk and South Gardens', also called the South Terrace, which continue westwards the line of the Moss Walk, were completed in 1855 with the alcove at its western end finished in 1857. In 1858, a stone portico was added to the north front of the house, outside the Tribes Room.

From 1861 onwards, as part of a major overhaul of the water supply to Erddig, a new hydraulic ram was installed. As well as supplying water to the house, it also powered two new fountains, with terracotta basins, supplied by Blashfield's of Stamford. These were the centrepieces of Phillips' new formal garden. A set of wide stone steps and balustrades were added to the east front entrance of the house in 1863.

The next head gardener, Alexander Stirton, introduced rhododendrons and many of the richly coloured flowering shrubs favoured by the Victorians. The Erddig garden reached its apogee in the late nineteenth century. In 1909 the *Journal of Horticulture and Cottage Garden* described the little flower garden to the south of the central walk, which contained a mixed planting of *Rosa* 'Dorothy Perkins' and *Clematis* × *jackmanii*, growing with variegated Box Elder (*Acer negundo* 'Variegatum'). About three years later Philip Yorke II added Dutch gables to the pavilions that flank the Victorian parterre, as a deliberate bow to the Dutch origins of John Meller's garden. This was to be the

Thomas Pritchard, Gardener (b.1762/3), painted in 1830 (Servants' Hall)

last enrichment. In 1914 the gardeners left for the Western Front and many did not come back. Erddig never recovered.

As the house decayed under Simon Yorke IV, the garden ran to seed. By the 1950s the Garden House, which had been home to generations of Erddig gardeners, was in a state of near collapse. Graham Stuart Thomas, the Trust's Gardens Adviser, described the scene in the early 1970s:

The only gardeners were sheep; at least they kept much of the grass mown, but did not tackle the nettles. They were much favoured by Mr Yorke for not only did they do the rough mowing but also helped him to control the yew trees.

Yet the skeleton of the early eighteenth-century garden could still be made out beneath the nettles, and so the Trust decided after further research to undertake a three-year-long campaign of restoration, which was carried out by a team under Mike Snowden, the first head gardener at Erddig since Albert Gillam had left in despair. The following tour describes the results of that work. A separate garden leaflet is also available.

TOUR OF THE GARDEN

THE PARTERRE

The present layout is largely Edwardian, although the fountains were installed in 1861, and at about the same time the walls were altered to reveal more of the house from the garden. The cusped gables were superimposed on the side walls around 1912, when the clock was brought from nearby Stansty Park. The walls are clothed with climbing roses, ceanothus and clematis. Nearby are Mexican Orange Blossom (*Choisya ternata*), *Magnolia cylindrica* and *Illicium henryi*. The beds are planted in two styles; foliage beds containing Cotton Lavender (*Santolina chamaecyparissus*) and Black Lily-grass (*Ophiopogon planiscapus* 'Nigresceus'), and the L-shaped beds, edged with blue-grey grass (*Festuca glauca*) but planted for summer displays with annuals, tender perennials and, in springtime, bulbs. This type of annual bedding developed during the mid-nineteenth century following extensive plant introductions from South Africa and southern and central America.

THE AXIAL WALK

The two vases at each end of the top path stand on cheese presses once used on the estate farms. Near the two central vases is a sundial which the Yorkes twisted round in spring and autumn to conform to British Summer Time. Along either side of the path are clipped mushrooms of Portugal Laurel (*Prunus lusitanica*), a hardy tree. These are surrounded by false boxes in the style used at Versailles. The laurels mimic orange trees and other tender shrubs that would be grown in winter houses or orangeries. The Gothic sandstone pinnacles between the laurels came from St Giles church, Wrexham.

THE ROSE GARDEN

This secluded garden, with its curved beds, contains many interesting shrubs, trees and climbing roses, including Black Mulberry (*Morus nigra*), *Cornus controversa* 'Variegata', *Lonicera syringantha* and young specimens of *Quercus* × *turneri*. A double-stemmed Silver Birch (*Betula pendula*) was tapped by the Yorkes, who used its sap in wine-making.

The view east from the house towards the canal and gate-screen

THE WEST FRONT

One of the most original features of the park laid out by William Emes is the Cylindrical Cascade, which can be seen about a quarter of a mile north west of the house. The Afon Ddu gathers in a circular stone basin with a cylindrical weir at its centre and exits through a tunnel a few yards away. This was designed to prevent the erosion of the river bed and banks by lowering the level of the stream quickly.

THE FRUIT TREES

The replanting of 1975–7 followed, wherever practicable, the 1718 lists of fruit trees. To these old varieties of plums, pears, peaches, apricots and vines were added other ancient or rare varieties of fruit, trained as espaliers or fans; even their names are mouth-watering: Pitmaston Pine Apple, Fenouillet Rouge, Autumn Bergamot, Nonpareil. Around the bases of these trees is planted a collection of old daffodil and narcissus varieties given by the National Trust for Scotland from their garden at Threave; a further collection was given by the Rosewarne Experimental Horticulture Station at Camborne, Cornwall. Apples are not mentioned in the lists of fruit formerly grown on the walls, suggesting that they formed the main orchard blocks shown on Badeslade's engraving. These blocks, underplanted with the Pheasant's Eye Narcissus (*Narcissus poeticus* var. *recurvus*), have been reproduced using eighteenth- and nineteenth-century varieties. The fruit is used in the tea-room and is occasionally for sale.

THE WALL BORDERS

As well as ancient fruit varieties, the garden walls support many other wall plants, including the Blue Potato Vine (*Solanum crispum* 'Glasnevin'), the orange honeysuckle (*Lonicera* × *brownii*), yellow honeysuckle (*Lonicera tragophylla*), roses, clematis and the pink-flowered jasmine (*Jasminum* × *stephanense*). The borders are planted with summer-flowering herbaceous plants, to which are added annuals and tender perennials

THE PLEACHED LIMES

Double avenues of pleached limes (*Tilia × euchlora*) mark the position of the original garden walls demolished in the eighteenth century. Trained trees and hedges were a popular feature of the seventeenth- and eighteenth-century gardens. It was possible to walk between these raised hedges or beneath bowers in the cool and shade, yet still view the garden between the stems or through 'windows' cut in the hedges. The mature double avenues of limes (*Tilia × europaea*) flanking the canal are thought also to have once been pleached.

THE FISHPOND

A large Swamp Cypress (*Taxodium distichum*) dominates the area near the Golden Gates that lead to Big Wood, west of the pond. Other trees here include a Weeping Ash (*Fraxinus excelsior* 'Pendula'). Tulip Tree (*Liriodendron tulipiferum*), *Sorbus cashmiriana* and Oriental Hawthorn (*Crataegus laciniata*). On Badeslade's plan of 1739, the pond is shown walled or hedged. East of the pond is the sundial engraved with Meller's coat of arms. Surrounding it, a curious pattern of yew hedges (*Taxus baccata*) has been replanted according to Badeslade's engraving, replacing an overgrown nineteenth-century rose garden.

THE CANAL AND SCREEN

The wrought-iron screen, gates and overthrow at the end of the canal were bought from Stansty Park in 1908 and erected after repair by Joseph Wright, the Erddig blacksmith. They are attributed to Robert Davies, who is known to have also supplied wrought iron to Erddig in the 1720s (see p.33). The twin mounds on either side of the screen were formed of dredgings from the canal and were the site of a former bridge and boathouse built by estate men *c.*1904.

THE MOSS WALK

The Queen Anne gates were a present to Simon III and Victoria Yorke from his brother, John. This wall is planted with a collection of ivy cultivars. Erddig holds this collection for the National Council for the Conservation of Plants and Gardens.

A cordoned pear in the garden

THE VICTORIAN GARDEN AND YEW WALK

The trees in the avenue of Irish Yew (*Taxus baccata* 'Fastigiata') were overgrown and unclipped when the National Trust took over the garden. They were cut down to two feet in the winter of 1975–6 and have now regrown to their intended size and shape. Flanking the Yew Walk are Dwarf Box (*Buxus sempervirens* 'Suffruticosa') hedges in a chain design after a pattern seen by Simon and Victoria Yorke at Versailles, and a collection of holly (*Iex sp.*) cultivars. These are planted on the site of a former line of variegated hollies; one remaining tree can be seen at either end.

THE HERB BORDER AND DRYING GREEN

Nearly 60 different herbs can be seen here. Herbs were of great importance to a household such as Erddig; they were used in cooking, laid amongst clothes to deter moths, and formed the basis of the medicine chest. Opposite is the Drying Green, where, after washing, linen and clothes would be laid out to dry and bleach in the sun. It is now planted with a collection of cob nuts and fruit trees, including medlar (*Mespilus germanica*), Cornelian Cherry (*Cornus mas*), damson, walnut and quince (*Cydonia oblonga*). To the left is the early eighteenth-century dovecot, which houses a flock of fantails.

CHAPTER EIGHT
THE ESTATE

The Erddig estate is a lowland agricultural estate of woodlands, meadows, marsh and rivers which today provide an important buffer of rural land on the urban fringe of Wrexham. Of the 1,800 or so acres which came to the National Trust in 1973, 1,500 acres are still let on agricultural tenancies, many of the farms having formed part of the estate since the early eighteenth century. In its heyday the estate was almost entirely self-supporting, with the farms, cottages, mills and network of roads, paths, bridges and fences being built and maintained by the workforce of labourers and craftsmen.

The owners of Erddig relied heavily on their stewards or land agents, whose ledgers, account books, rentals and correspondence provide a vivid record of how the estate was managed between the

late seventeenth and twentieth centuries. During his imprisonment for debt Joshua Edisbury's creditors continued to press him for repayment. However, his loyal steward John Williams frequently managed to borrow money for his master and regularly sent woodcock, hares, geese, butter and cheese produced on the estate to his prison cell. Eventually, Williams was obliged to depart, hiring himself to a Mr Leighton: 'Tho: I left Erthigg God knows it was with a hevy heart for I had not inclination to leave yor Service and my leaving it was more upon force than choyce'.

Following Edisbury's bankruptcy, the estate was on the market for several years, the demesne of Erddig being tenanted by the Rev. Thomas Holland between 1713 and 1715. Edisbury's accounts show that in 1716 the entire estate yielded an annual rental income of £1,800. To confirm this figure and to ascertain any potential competition from neighbouring landowners, with characteristic thoroughness John Meller commissioned an 'Exact Survey' of the estate from John Humphreys before he acquired it. (The survey is dated 1713, but was probably not completed until c.1716.) It contains a schematic plan of the Erddig demesne, given as about 114 acres. The estate buildings included a cow-house and coach-house of twelve bays, with a cow-yard 40 × 30 yards, and a stable block of eight bays, as well as a brew-house, slaughter-house, wash-house, kiln and dog kennel. Water was provided by a forcing pump and carried to the kitchen and house by means of lead pipes. The survey also provides an extraordinarily detailed record of the 52 individual drafts (or tenements) forming the estate. Some of the individual fields, enclosing ridge and furrow, can still be seen in what is now the south park. The fields were evocatively named, with such titles as 'Little Fair Oak Field', 'Milking Bank', 'The Clover Field' and 'The Great Castle Field', the last so-called

86

called after its proximity to the ancient motte and bailey above the Afon Ddu.

In 1716 Bryn Golan (now known as Bryn Goleu tenement), to the south of the present park, was leased for life to the 81-year-old Frances Williams, the lease including 'some duties of work in harvest, some coal carrying and the keeping of a dog'. The annual rent on the 34-acre plot was £10. The sixteenth-century house that came with it still survives, although it has been substantially altered since 1715 by the addition of bay, dormer and oriel windows and a two-storey wing. A wide variety of

tenants has occupied the house since that time: at the end of the eighteenth century, Robert Lloyd, a retired London grocer, was living there, while in the mid-nineteenth century it was rented, along with Hafod-y-Bwch farm, for £214 per annum to a Sarah Matthews.

Some tenanted land occupied the river valley bottoms and was greatly affected by the floodwaters of the Afon Ddu and the Clywedog. In 1715 parts of the Clywedog itself had become so silted up that in places it was less than five inches deep. At times of flood it regularly broke its banks and damaged the

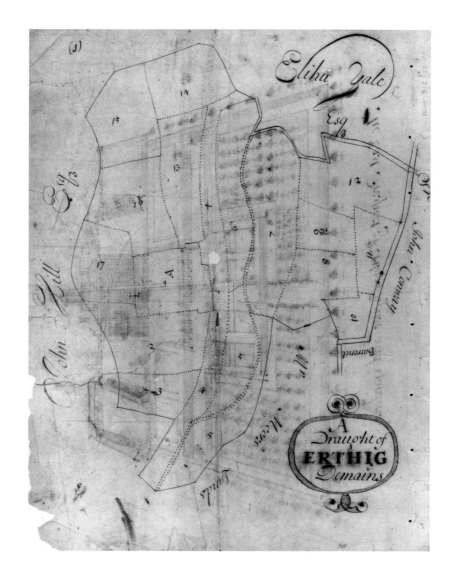

(Opposite)
Jack Henshaw,
Gamekeeper (b.1731/2);
by John Walters, 1791
(Servants' Hall)

(Right) The c.1713 map
of the Erddig estate

adjacent fields. In 1713 Humphreys reported that 'one field is this year wheat and very good but in great danger of spoiling by the good river, besides the said river for want of scouring is so bad that will scarce carry enough of water to send to Kingmill'.

There had been a grinding mill at the confluence of the Gwenfro and Clywedog rivers since the fourteenth century. In 1634 the Kingsmill became an outlying part of the estate when it was acquired by Joshua Edisbury's grandfather, Kendrick. Kendrick Edisbury had much surplus cash to invest, and between 1627 and his death in 1638 bought a number of properties in the Marchwiel, Pickhill, Esclusham and Ruabon townships which were later to form parts of the Erddig estate.

The tenant farmers of Wrexham were compelled by law to grind their corn and malt at the Kingsmill, but business was increasingly poached by rival mills. The proliferation of illegal querns (hand mills) and horse mills in Wrexham in the 1660s was only temporarily halted by court action. As early as 1715 Meller was repairing the water courses and fabric of the Kingsmill, and was determined to assert his rights to the lucrative income from it – almost £100 per annum in tolls. In 1716 he purchased a set of twenty weights from the Exchequer Court of Receipt for measuring milled corn; these can now be seen in the Dining Room.

On inheriting the estate in 1767, Philip Yorke I decided to rebuild the Kingsmill, at a cost of £1,000. The new mill, which still stands (now owned by Wrexham Borough Council), was built on more or less the same site. Although the work was directed by the millwright with the help of local craftsmen, the bulk of the labour was provided by up to twelve of the estate workmen. Work began in December 1768 and was completed in 1770, with two new millstones being acquired for £13 in June 1771.

In January–March 1769 Philip Yorke also diverted the course of the Clywedog to provide a more reliable water source and to protect the land identified in the 1715 survey as being constantly damaged by flooding. In order to reduce competition, he acquired the rival Puleston mill and ancillary buildings as well as 40 acres of land and adapted these to form a farmhouse and outbuildings

for the Kingsmill estate, which he rented at an enhanced figure of £240 per annum. Nevertheless, by 1774 illegal malt mills and horse mills had proliferated to such an extent that business was suffering. The Kingsmill's monopoly of milling in Wrexham was finally broken in 1854, when 29 influential innkeepers, brewers, maltsters, millers, flour dealers and auctioneers formed an association to resist what they claimed were illegal tolls. Steam-driven mills were built in Wrexham, close to the railway, with which the Kingsmill was unable to compete. It struggled on until 1940, when it finally closed.

During the 1770s Philip Yorke I invested a substantial portion of his Hutton inheritance in the estate, creating a new estate yard and stables in 1772–4. In 1772–5 William Emes was employed to level the water meadows at Frenchmill, in the north part of the estate near Coed-y-Glyn. Between 1777 and 1781 he also redirected the river below the west front of the house, filling in its old course, which had originally run through a lake known as the engine pond. He also removed the field boundaries, transforming what had been an agricultural landscape into parkland.

In 1773 Philip I bought the neighbouring Sontley estate of 146 acres for £7,900, and between 1777 and 1781 had Emes construct the Sontley weir, partly to solve the problems of flooding on the Sontley road and bridge, which connected it to Erddig. The seventeenth-century house at Sontley, which is visible on the horizon in Badeslade's bird's-eye view, was not dissimilar to Erddig. It was demolished in the 1760s–70s, and a new house, now known as New Sontley Farm, was formed from the original coach-house and stabling in the nineteenth century. Dressed stone quoins incorporated into the Erddig garden walls may have been salvaged from the demolition of the old house. In 1776 Philip I acquired the smaller Hafod y Bwch estate for £1,200 and modernised its farm buildings; one includes a date-stone for 1800 bearing his initials. The farmhouse itself was rebuilt by the Yorkes in the nineteenth century.

Elizabeth Yorke took as active an interest in the running of the estate as her husband. She was particularly concerned with the efficiency of the dairy, and in April 1773 wrote to John Caesar, 'I wish my dairy to produce more plentifully, the quantity of butter does not sound much for eight cows'. In May the following year she requested that, when 'the cheeses are begun to be made, I would have you send the number that were made in the week'. Large stone cheese presses still survive at Manor Farm, the model farm built on the estate in the nineteenth century. The dairy itself, also called the China House, was sited some way to the north-east of Erddig. It was reached by a path leading down to the river from the wooded escarpment, suggesting that it was meant to be both a decorative and a functional building: in 1784 Lord Torrington thought it 'out of all character, having never held one bowl of milk'. Although the northern part contained a room covered with glazed tiles, the southern end, known as the Meadow House, was used as a cottage. In 1830 it was occupied by Edward Barnes the woodman, but it may also have been the cottage used by the park-keepers John Hammer (in 1851) and John Morris (in 1861). By 1883, however, it had become the home of another estate wood-man, William Hughes.

Life on the Erddig farm did not always run smoothly. When a number of turkeys escaped from the poultry yard in the early 1770s and made their way to the neighbouring Sontley estate, Elizabeth Yorke complained to John Caesar:

I think the workmen were very blamable for offering to carry fowls out of the garden without first applying to you . . . I suppose with the intent of gaining a draft of ale. . . . I feel that this incident shows rather a want of care in my kitchen maid and dairy maid for I doubt they did not know the stock of my poultry yard.

Caesar was sent by his mistress to retrieve the birds.

Weekly returns for the Erddig staff indicate the scale of activities on the estate in the 1770s. Between 11 and 18 October 1778, three men were employed each day carting lime, stones and earth for the improvements being implemented by Emes. From nine to twelve people were employed on the farm; eight in the kitchen garden and pleasure grounds; between two and five in the hot-house and woods, and between five and six on repairs. Philip Yorke I attempted to be a fair employer. In 1772 he told Caesar:

I am very willing and always desirous that my constant workmen should derive from me every comfort and reasonable advantage and I am Happy to allow and set

The Dairy, or China House

apart for every year (whilst it is to be found) a Part of my Field for the Planting of Potatoes to supply them in Winter but I must insist that when such Piece of Ground is chalked out, they be strictly cautioned to abstain from cutting and pruning such young *trees* as I may grow thereon.

In 1807, shortly after he inherited Erddig, Simon Yorke II commissioned a new survey of his estate. This now amounted to 2,593 acres, of which he had 245 acres in hand, the rest being tenanted. In the same year he acquired Erddig Fechan, or Little Erddig, an estate on the western boundary of the park. The house had been built in 1510 and from the middle of the sixteenth century had been the seat of the Erthyg family, who in the seventeenth century had owned parts of the Erddig estate from which they took their name.

Simon II and his son, Simon III, consolidated and

Ned Humphreys, who was a gamekeeper on the estate from 1866 until 1871, when he died of TB aged 24

maintained the estate, in particular by establishing new woodland plantations over a 30-year period. Trees were planted to the north in Coed-y-Glyn in 1844–5 and at Bryn Cabanau in 1870. To the east Forest Wood was laid out between 1833 and 1839, and Sontley Field replanted in 1833. To the south and west, Cae Coch was planted in 1849 and Hafod in 1858. At the same time mature timber was being felled and sold: in 1839 Edward Hughes and John Jones were paid for felling at a rate of 8d for small trees, 2s for middle-sized trees and 3s for large trees. Much of the timber was tranported out of the woods on the hybrid timber wagon now in the estate yard. The large lime and beech trees, some of which may have been planted by Simon I in the 1740s, fetched £6 each.

The estate was bringing in an annual income of £3,634 6s 7d from rents by 1840, when the Yorkes were making further improvements to the tenanted properties. In 1838, for example, a new coach-house, saddle room and stables were built at Coed-y-Glyn. Forest Lodge was put up at the eastern boundary of the park in 1854, and a double lodge at Plas Grono in 1859, probably to coincide with the creation of a new carriage drive through the south park and a bridge at Bryn Goleu. The drive from Forest Lodge was opened on New Year's Day 1864.

In the late nineteenth century Simon Yorke III carried out extensive repairs to and modernisation of the tenanted farms. The most ambitious was the construction of Manor Farm, built between March 1884 and September 1886 at a cost of £2,226. This red-brick model farm included extensive outbuildings – cow-house, cart sheds, stable and granary – and was designed to replace Little Erddig, which Simon III demolished in 1886 following a fire. Some of the panelling was rescued and reused at Erddig in what is now the White Bedroom. New farmhouses and outbuildings were also erected at Pont-y-ffrwyd (1888–90), Sontley (1891–2) and Pentre Clawdd (1896); and ten new houses constructed in Ruabon (1886–7).

At Erddig itself, Philip Yorke II installed a hydraulic ram in 1899, made by John Blake Ltd of Accrington. The 'B' ram used the power of the Black Brook to work a pump which drew pure spring water at a rate of 10,000 gallons per day up

Erddig from Bersham colliery (now closed)

90 feet to storage cisterns in the roof of the house. The regular thud of the pump mechanism became known as the 'heart of Erddig'. Water was also supplied to Bryn Goleu and New Sontley Farm in this manner. The system was renewed in 1923 and still provides water for the garden fountains.

In 1908 Philip II's agent, Mr Capper, announced:

Mr Yorke, having for several years allowed anyone who so desired to walk along many of the private roads on the estate in the vicinity of the residence, feels bound to withdraw the privilege for the future as it has recently been abused, serious damage has been done to the gates and fences, and to the tenants' and other stock.

The Wrexham community objected strongly, particularly because local miners had used these roads on their way to and from the Bersham colliery for the previous 20 years. Following an outcry in the local press and representations from the Mayor of Wrexham, Philip Yorke agreed to reinstate the rights of way.

Mining had been an important part of the estate

since the seventeenth century. In the 1690s Joshua Edisbury had works at Trelogan and Gop, which extracted copper, lead and iron ore. In 1719 Meller worked two pits at Bryn-yr-Owen: 'The Old Pitt' and 'The New Pitt' brought in an average profit of £3–4 per week in 1719. In April 1721 Richard Jones, Meller's agent, wrote, 'We go on sinking for coale as fast as wee can', and by May 1722 he reported that 'Upon Saturday evening the Colliers worked thro the Coale which is 2½ yards thicke and to be shure as good a Coale as any in the north wales'. By 1728 coal was being supplied from the estate's pits to 77 individuals, including the publicans of the Red Lion, White Lion and Mitre, as well as the local clockmaker, glover and dyer. By the 1790s Philip Yorke I was granting leases for mining in return for a rental income and usually a sixth of all the coal dug. Each week a cart from Bersham colliery delivered coal to Erddig. In 1904 the house itself consumed over 118 tons, with a further 60 tons being supplied to the sawmill, stableyard, blacksmith's shop and laundry in the estate yard.

By the early 1920s the estate was not so financially buoyant. In 1903 Philip II had warned his agent, Mr Williams, 'Allow me to draw your attention again to the necessity of curtailing expenses as I may say with the prospect of a decreased royalty from the Vauxhall colliery, the present staff can not be maintained'. In 1920 Philip had begun to sell outlying parts of the estate, and this continued in 1922 following his death with sales of farmland at Ponty-ffrwyd, Pentre Mallyn, Tan-y-Llan and Maes-y-Llan, as well as building plots.

Philip had hoped that his son, Simon IV, would be advised and supported by Willy Gittins, the estate foreman's son, whom he saw as a potential agent. However, Gittins left Erddig to go into business on his own, and Simon fell out with the agent dealing with the tenanted farms. Simon refused to sell further land to raise capital; indeed he was determined to keep the estate intact. However, he lacked both the will and the money to modernise or even maintain the numerous buildings on the estate. During the severe agricultural depression of the 1930s, many rapidly became derelict as they fell out of use. After 1947 they also suffered from the

Bryn Goleu

mining subsidence that did so much damage to the house.

After Philip Yorke III inherited in 1966, he gradually began to turn the tide with the help of his agent, Mr Kitching. Inevitably, efforts had to be concentrated on saving the house and its contents, and by the time the Trust took over in 1973, several of the estate buildings, such as the eighteenth-century lodge at Coed-y-Glyn, were beyond repair and had to be demolished. However, many of the dead or dying trees in the park have been replaced. A new flood relief channel was constructed along what had been the old course of the river below the west front, before Emes diverted it. The estate cottages built on the site of Plas Grono were converted into accommodation for National Trust volunteers, who continue to help with the maintenance of the park. The estate now supports important wildlife habitats: Hafod Wood is managed by the North Wales Naturalists Trust and the marshes of Sontley are designated a Site of Special Scientific Interest.

The rescue of Erddig captured the imagination and enthusiasm of many people, and the property continues to be supported by the many visitors who come each year and the community of volunteers who assist in a wide variety of work. However, the endowment, considered sufficient 20 years ago, has dwindled in value, and the National Trust, like the Yorkes before it, faces increasing pressure in meeting the costs of repairs and maintenance to the buildings and land throughout the estate.

FAMILY TREE OF THE YORKES

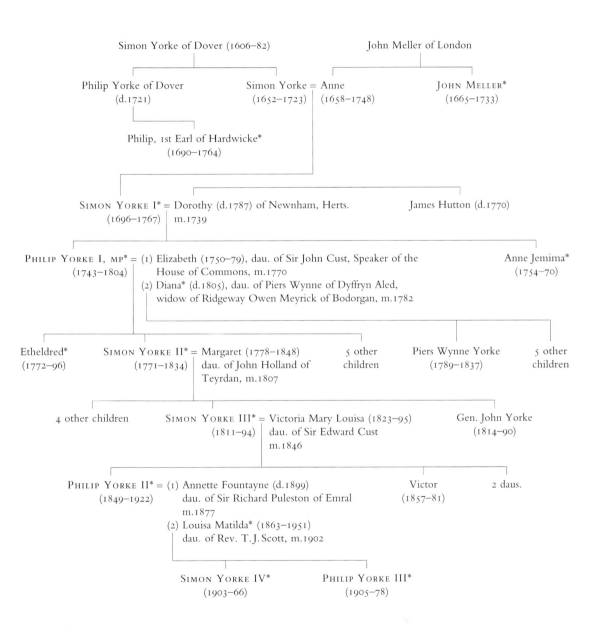

Simon Yorke of Dover (1606–82)   John Meller of London

Philip Yorke of Dover (d.1721)   Simon Yorke (1652–1723) = Anne (1658–1748)   JOHN MELLER* (1665–1733)

Philip, 1st Earl of Hardwicke* (1690–1764)

SIMON YORKE I* (1696–1767) = Dorothy (d.1787) of Newnham, Herts. m.1739   James Hutton (d.1770)

PHILIP YORKE I, MP* (1743–1804) = (1) Elizabeth (1750–79), dau. of Sir John Cust, Speaker of the House of Commons, m.1770
(2) Diana* (d.1805), dau. of Piers Wynne of Dyffryn Aled, widow of Ridgeway Owen Meyrick of Bodorgan, m.1782   Anne Jemima* (1754–70)

Etheldred* (1772–96)   SIMON YORKE II* (1771–1834) = Margaret (1778–1848) dau. of John Holland of Teyrdan, m.1807   5 other children   Piers Wynne Yorke (1789–1837)   5 other children

4 other children   SIMON YORKE III* (1811–94) = Victoria Mary Louisa (1823–95) dau. of Sir Edward Cust m.1846   Gen. John Yorke (1814–90)

PHILIP YORKE II* (1849–1922) = (1) Annette Fountayne (d.1899) dau. of Sir Richard Puleston of Emral m.1877
(2) Louisa Matilda* (1863–1951) dau. of Rev. T.J.Scott, m.1902   Victor (1857–81)   2 daus.

SIMON YORKE IV* (1903–66)   PHILIP YORKE III* (1905–78)

Owners of Erddig are shown in CAPITALS

* denotes a portrait in the house

BIBLIOGRAPHY

The vast archive of Yorke family papers has been deposited at Hawarden in the Flintshire Record Office, which has produced a three-volume catalogue of the collection.

Cust, Albinia Lucy, *Chronicles of Erthig on the Dyke*, 2 vols, 1914.

Dennis, Nigel, *Cards of Identity*, 1955.

Drury, Martin, 'Early Eighteenth-century Furniture at Erddig', *Apollo*, July 1978, pp. 46–55.

Hardy, John, Sheila Landy, and Charles D. Wright, *A State Bed for Erthig*, Victoria & Albert Museum, 1972.

Hine, Reginald L., *The Manor of Newnham* [1910].

Jackson-Stops, Gervase, 'Erddig Park', *Country Life*, clxiii, 6, 13, 20 April 1978, pp. 906–9, 970–3, 1070–4.

Jackson-Stops, Gervase, *An English Arcadia*, 1992, pp. 48–50.

Jourdain, Margaret, 'Furniture at Erddig', *Country Life*, lxvii, 22 March 1930, pp. 441, 623.

Jourdain, Margaret, 'Erthig' *Country Life*, lxviii, 16, 23 August 1930, pp. 206, 234.

Knox-Mawer, Howard, 'Last Days at Erthig', *Anglo-Welsh Review*, xxvi, no. 57, autumn 1976, pp. 170–6.

Loveday, John, *Diary of a Tour in 1732*, 1890, pp. 79–81.

Mallet, J. V. G., 'Pottery and Porcelain at Erddig', *Apollo*, July 1978, pp. 40–5.

Mars-Jones, Adam, *Lantern Lecture*, 1981.

'Nimrod' [Charles Apperley], *My Life and Times*, 1927 [reprinted from *Fraser's Magazine*, 1842].

Tipping, H. Avray, *English Homes*, period iv, i, 1920, p. 179.

Veysey, A. Geoffrey, 'Philip Yorke, Last Squire of Erddig', *Transactions of the Denbighshire Historical Society*, pp. 121–36.

Vyvvian, David, 'Survey of Erthig, 1715', *Transactions of the Denbighshire Historical Society*, xviii, 1969.

Waterson, Merlin, 'Servants at Erddig', *Country Life*, 19 February, 16 September 1976; 22 September, 13 October 1977; 5, 26 October 1978.

Waterson, Merlin, 'Elihu Yale', *The Smithsonian*, October 1977.

Waterson, Merlin, 'Elizabeth Ratcliffe: An Artistic Lady's Maid', *Apollo*, July 1978, pp. 56–63.

Waterson, Merlin, *The Servants' Hall: A Domestic History of Erddig*, 1980.

Yorke, Louisa, *Facts and Fancies*, 1923.

A fragment of early eighteenth-century wallpaper recently uncovered at Erddig

INDEX